Certified Information System Security Professional (CISSP)

Practice Questions

Version 1

[Document Control]

Proposal Name	:	CISSP – Practice Questions
Document Version	:	1.0
Document Release Date	:	18 September 2018
Reference	:	IPSpecialist_PQ_CISSP_v1.0

Feedback:

If you have any comments regarding the quality of this book, or otherwise alter it to better suit your needs, you can contact us through email at info@ipspecialist.net

Please make sure to include the book title and ISBN in your message

About IPSpecialist

IPSPECIALIST LTD. IS COMMITTED TO EXCELLENCE AND DEDICATED TO YOUR SUCCESS.

Our philosophy is to treat our customers like family. We want you to succeed, and we are willing to do anything possible to help you make it happen. We have the proof to back up our claims. We strive to accelerate billions of careers with great courses, accessibility, and affordability. We believe that continuous learning and knowledge evolution are most important things to keep re-skilling and up-skilling the world.

Planning and creating a specific goal is where IPSpecialist helps. We can create a career track that suits your visions as well as develop the competencies you need to become a professional Network Engineer. We can also assist you with the execution and evaluation of proficiency level based on the career track you choose, as they are customized to fit your specific goals.

We help you STAND OUT from the crowd through our detailed IP training content packages.

Course Features:

- *Self-Paced learning*
    - O Learn at your own pace and in your own time
- *Covers Complete Exam Blueprint*
    - O Prep-up for the exam with confidence
- *Case Study Based Learning*
    - O Relate the content with real life scenarios
- *Subscriptions that suits you*
    - O Get more pay less with IPS Subscriptions
- *Career Advisory Services*
    - O Let industry experts plan your career journey
- *Virtual Labs to test your skills*
    - O With IPS vRacks, you can testify your exam preparations
- *Practice Questions*
    - O Practice Questions to measure your preparation standards
- *On Request Digital Certification*
    - O On request digital certification from IPSpecialist LTD.

About the Authors:

This book has been compiled with the help of multiple professional engineers. These engineers specialize in different fields e.g Networking, Security, Cloud, Big Data, IoT etc. Each engineer develops content in its specialized field that is compiled to form a comprehensive certification guide.

About the Technical Reviewers:

Nouman Ahmed Khan

AWS-Architect, CCDE, CCIEX5 (R&S, SP, Security, DC, Wireless), CISSP, CISA, CISM is a Solution Architect working with a major telecommunication provider in Qatar. He works with enterprises, mega-projects, and service providers to help them select the best-fit technology solutions. He also works closely as a consultant to understand customer business processes and helps select an appropriate technology strategy to support business goals. He has more than 14 years of experience working in Pakistan/Middle-East & UK. He holds a Bachelor of Engineering Degree from NED University, Pakistan, and M.Sc. in Computer Networks from the UK.

Abubakar Saeed

Abubakar Saeed has more than twenty-five years of experience, Managing, Consulting, Designing, and implementing large-scale technology projects, extensive experience heading ISP operations, solutions integration, heading Product Development, Presales, and Solution Design. Emphasizing on adhering to Project timelines and delivering as per customer expectations, he always leads the project in the right direction with his innovative ideas and excellent management.

Muhammad Yusuf

Muhammad Yousuf is a professional technical content writer. He is Cisco Certified Network Associate in Routing and Switching, holding bachelor's degree in Telecommunication Engineering from Sir Syed University of Engineering and Technology. He has both technical knowledge and industry sounding information, which he uses perfectly in his career.

Become an author & earn with us

If you are interested in becoming an author & want to earn with one time effort. IPS Offers "Earn with us" program for authors & students who have insights on IT related content & want to expand their reach globally can apply for the program here: www.ipspecialist.net/ews

Table of Contents

Our Products

Technology Workbooks

IPSpecialist Technology workbooks are the ideal guides to developing the hands-on skills necessary to pass the exam. Our workbook covers official exam blueprint and explains the technology with real life case study based labs. The content covered in each workbook consists of individually focused technology topics presented in an easy-to-follow, goal-oriented, step-by-step approach. Every scenario features detailed breakdowns and thorough verifications to help you completely understand the task and associated technology.

We extensively used mind maps in our workbooks to visually explain the technology. Our workbooks have become a widely used tool to learn and remember the information effectively.

vRacks

Our highly scalable and innovative virtualized lab platforms let you practice the IP Specialist Technology Workbook at your own time and your own place as per your convenience.

Quick Reference Sheets

Our quick reference sheets are a concise bundling of condensed notes of the complete exam blueprint for CISSP. It's an ideal handy document to help you remember the most important technology concepts related to CISSP exam.

Practice Questions

IP Specialists' Practice Questions are dedicatedly designed for certification exam perspective. The collection of these questions from our technology workbooks are prepared to keep the exam blueprint in mind covering not only important but necessary topics as well. It's an ideal document to practice and revise your certification.

About the CISSP Exam

CISSP Linear Examination Information

Length of exam:	6 hours
Number of questions:	250
Question format:	Multiple choice and advanced innovative questions
Passing grade:	700 out of 1000 points
Exam language availability:	French, German, Brazilian Portuguese, Spanish, Japanese, Simplified Chinese, Korean
Testing centre:	(ISC)2 Authorized PPC and PVTC Select Pearson VUE

The Certified Information Systems Security Professional (CISSP) is the most globally recognized certification in the information security market. CISSP validates an information security professional's deep technical and managerial knowledge and experience to effectively design, engineer, and manage the overall security posture of an organization.

The broad spectrum of topics included in the CISSP Common Body of Knowledge (CBK) ensures its relevancy across all disciplines in the field of information security. Successful candidates are competent in the following 8 domains:

1. Security and Risk Management
2. Asset Security
3. Security Architecture and Engineering
4. Communication and Network Security
5. Identity and Access Management (IAM)
6. Security Assessment and Testing
7. Security Operations
8. Software Development Security

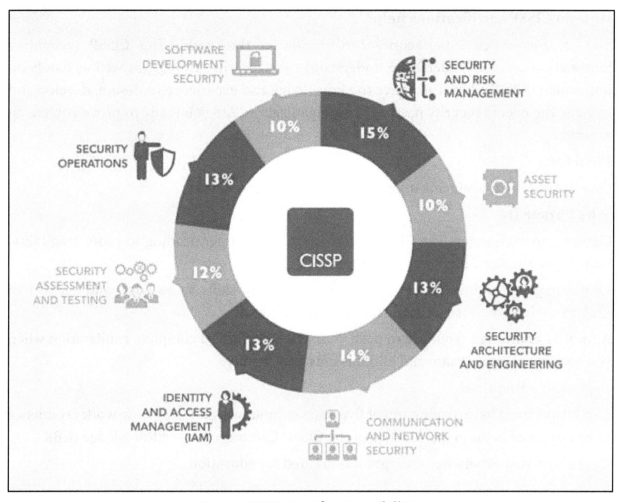

Figure 1 CISSP Certifications Skill Matrix

Experience Requirements

Candidates must have a minimum of 5 years cumulative paid full-time work experience in 2 or more of the 8 domains of the CISSP CBK. Earning a 4-year college degree or regional equivalent or an additional credential from the (ISC)² approved list will satisfy 1 year of the required experience. Education credit will only satisfy 1 year of experience.

A candidate that doesn't have the required experience to become a CISSP may become an Associate of (ISC)² by successfully passing the CISSP examination. The Associate of (ISC)² will then have 6 years to earn the 5 years required experience.

Accreditation

CISSP was the first credential in the field of information security to meet the stringent requirements of ANSI/ ISO/IEC Standard 17024.

How do CISSP certifications help?

The most-esteemed cybersecurity certification in the world. The CISSP recognizes information security leaders who understand cybersecurity strategy, as well as hands-on implementation. It shows you have the knowledge and experience to design, develop and manage the overall security posture of an organization. Are you ready to prove you are an expert?

Ideal for:

Experienced, high-achieving information security professionals

Why Pursue It:

Career game-changer: The CISSP can catapult your career, leading to more credibility, better opportunities, higher pay and more.

Ongoing growth and learning: You will expand your skills, knowledge, and network of experts so that you can stay at the forefront of your craft.

A mighty challenge. You love to push yourself. You will feel complete exhilaration when you pass our rigorous exam and join this elite community.

Experience Required:

Candidates must have a minimum of five years cumulative, paid, full-time work experience in two or more of the eight domains of the CISSP Common Body of Knowledge (CBK).

Only a one-year experience exemption is granted for education.

(ISC)² Certifications

Information security careers can feel isolating! When you certify, you become a member of (ISC)² — a leading community of cybersecurity professionals. You can collaborate with thought leaders, network with global peers, expand your skills and so much more. It is a community that's here to support you throughout your career.

Figure 2 ISC² Certifications Track

Chapter 1: Security & Risk Management

1. Which of the following risk is related to confidentiality?

   A. Unauthorized disclosure
   B. Data modification
   C. Unavailability
   D. Repudiation

2. When two organizations decide to merge into a single organization, this organizational process is known as:

   A. Acquisition
   B. Divestiture
   C. Out-sourcing
   D. Upgrade

3. When a part of an organization is sold or separated; this organizational process is called:

   A. Acquisition
   B. Divestiture
   C. Out-sourcing
   D. Upgrade

4. Who is responsible for monitoring, motivation and directing the security committees.

   A. CSO
   B. Board of Directors
   C. Auditor
   D. IAO

5. Who is responsible for the protection of information assets?

   A. Chief Security Officer (CSO)
   B. Security Committee (SC)

C. Local Security Committee (LSC)

D. Information Asset Owners (IAOs)

6. When a user is redirected to a malicious website created by the attacker; this type of attack is known as

   A. Phishing

   B. Pharming

   C. SMS Phishing

   D. Cyber Stalking

7. When a user is lured to an attacker created an illegitimate website that looks similar to the actual website the user intended to visit; this type of attack is known as

   A. Phishing

   B. Pharming

   C. SMS Phishing

   D. Cyber Stalking

8. Transborder data flow is referred to as:
   A. Data across national borders
   B. Data across organizational borders
   C. Data across Network Zones
   D. None of the above

9. A unique symbol or mark that is used to represent an individual's or organization's product is known as:

   A. Copyright

   B. Trademark

   C. Patent

   D. Intellect Property

10. A type of risk assessment application that tries to assess qualitative and quantitative impacts on the business due to a disruptive event is called

   A. Business Impact Analysis (BIA)

  B. Business Continuity Planning (BCP)

  C. Risk Analysis

  D. Incident Management

11. Control that is designed for troubleshooting or identifying the error, issues, and irregularities is known as

  A. Preventive Control

  B. Detective Control

  C. Corrective Control

  D. None of the above

12. Which principals ensure the security policies enforced in an organization are meeting their goals and objectives

  A. Security Control Assessment (SCA)

  B. Risk Assessment

  C. Penetration Testing

  D. Audit

13. Intangible Assets in an information system are:

  A. Physical Assets

  B. Non-Physical Assets

  C. Both Physical & Non-physical

  D. None of the above

14. Which of the following is a threat modeling tool?

  A. SD Elements

  B. QRadar

  C. Wireshark

  D. Nessus

15. Which of the following is not a threat modeling methodology?

  A. STRIDE

  B. PASTA

C. TRIKE

D. VAST

E. None of the above

16. Which of the following is a threat modeling methodology by Microsoft?

A. STRIDE

B. PASTA

C. TRIKE

D. VAST

E. None of the above

17. You have been hired in a committee responsible for Scoping the risk & reviewing risk assessment and audit reports and approving significant changes to security policies and programs. What committee are you joining?

A. Security policy committee

B. Audit committee

C. Risk management committee

D. Security steering committee

18. What is the highest level of government data classification?

A. Confidential

B. Top secret

C. Sensitive

D. Secret

19. Identify the term related to the subject of the below options.

A. Database table

B. Readme.txt file

C. Authenticated user

D. 1099 Tax Form

20. Which canon of The (ISC)2® Code of Ethics should be considered the least important?

A. Protect society, the commonwealth, and the infrastructure

B. Advance and protect the profession

C. Act honorably, honestly, justly, responsibly, and legally

    D. Provide diligent and competent service to principals

21. Which of the following best describes COBIT?
    A. COBIT is a model for corporate governance.
    B. COBIT is a customizable framework for IT service management.
    C. COBIT provides a model for achieving business goals.
    D. COBIT is a model for IT governance.

22. Which of the following best describes ITIL?
    A. ITIL is a structure for providing best services in IT
    B. COBIT provides a framework for attaining business goals
    C. ITIL defines IT goals
    D. ITIL is a model for corporate governance

23. The Information Technology Infrastructure Library (ITIL) contains five sets of instructional steps. Which of the following is considered on new projects and focuses on making them operational IT services?
    A. Service Operation
    B. Service Design
    C. Service Transition
    D. Service Strategy

24. Many factors should be considered when assigning values to assets. Which of the following is not used to determine the value of an asset?
    A. The asset's value in the external marketplace
    B. The level of insurance required to cover the asset
    C. The initial and outgoing costs of purchasing, licensing and supporting the asset
    D. The asset's value to the organization's production operations

25. When developing a BCP, the amount of time it will be expected to take to get a device fixed and back into production related to the term.
    A. Mean time to repair
    B. Mean time between failures
    C. Maximum critical downtime
    D. Maximum tolerable downtime

26. Which of the following phase describe the actual starting planning of BCP?

    A. Reconstitution phase
    B. Recovery phase
    C. Project initiation phase
    D. Damage assessment phase

27. Which conducts after the BCP team has achieved management support?
    A. Business case
    B. Business impact analysis
    C. Risk analysis
    D. Threat report

28. Which one of the following steps come first in a Business Impact analysis?
    A. Calculate the risk for each different business function.
    B. Identify critical business functions.
    C. Create data-gathering techniques.
    D. Identify vulnerabilities and threats to business functions.

29. A business impact analysis works as functional analysis. Which of the following is not carried out during a business impact analysis?
    A. A parallel or full-interruption test
    B. The application of a classification scheme based on criticality levels
    C. The gathering of information through interviews
    D. Documentation of business functions

30. The NIST organization has outlined best practices for creating continuity plans. Which of the following phases deals with writing a policy that provides the guidance necessary to develop a Business Continuity Plan?
    A. Identify preventive controls.
    B. Develop the continuity planning policy statement.
    C. Create contingency strategies.
    D. Conduct the business impact analysis.

31. The integrity of data is not associated with which of the following?
    A. Unauthorized manipulation or changes to data
    B. The modification of data without authorization
    C. The extraction of data to share with unauthorized objects.
    D. The intentional or accidental substitution of data.

32. The confidentiality of data is linked to which of the following?
    A. Unauthorized manipulation or changes to data
    B. The modification of data without authorization
    C. The intentional or accidental substitution of data
    D. The extraction of data to share with unauthorized entities.

33. Which of the following is not involved in a risk assessment?
    A. Identifying assets
    B. Discontinuing activities that generate risk
    C. Identifying threats
    D. Analyzing risk concerning cost or criticality

34. A department manager has been asked to join a committee that is accountable for defining an acceptable level of risk for the organization, reviewing risk assessment and audit reports, and approving significant changes to security policies and programs. What committee is he joining?
    A. Security policy committee
    B. Audit committee
    C. Risk management committee
    D. Security regulating committee

35. Identify the basic method and their purpose to deal with risk?
    A. Risk transference. Share the risk with other entities.
    B. Risk reduction. Reduce the risk to an acceptable level.
    C. Risk rejection. Accept the current risk.
    D. Risk assignment. Assign risk to a specific owner.

36. With what phase of a business continuity plan does a company keep on when it is ready to move back into its original site or a new site?
    A. Damage assessment phase
    B. Recovery phase
    C. Reconstitution phase
    D. Project initiation phase

37. When implementing many security controls, including antivirus and antispam software, to protect the company's e-mail system. What type of approach is her company taking to handle the risk posed by the system?

    A. Risk mitigation

    B. Risk acceptance

    C. Risk avoidance

    D. Risk transference

38. Which of the following belongs to private-sector data classification?

    A. Public

    B. Secret

    C. Unclassified

    D. Sensitive but unclassified

39. Whose role is to observe security policies and procedures and provide reports to senior management about the effectiveness of security controls?

    A. Auditor

    B. Infosec security officer

    C. Users

    D. Data owners

40. Who has the functional responsibility of security?

    A. Auditor

    B. Users

    C. Infosec security officer

    D. Data owners

41. Concerning the classification of information, the levels of sensitivity used by the U.S. military include all the following except which one?

    A. Unclassified

    B. Confidential

    C. Controlled

    D. Secret

42. Which of the following is not the level of private-sector (commercial) data classification?

    A. Proprietary

    B. Classified

    C. Secret

    D. Confidential

43. Which of the following describes the process to remove complexity?
    A. Encryption
    B. Abstraction
    C. Obfuscation
    D. Data hiding

44. Which of the following describes the process of extracting only external properties to other components?
    A. Encryption
    B. Abstraction
    C. Obfuscation
    D. Data hiding

45. Which of the following does not belongs to an acceptable response to risk?
    A. Acceptance
    B. Reduction
    C. Displacement
    D. Transference

46. Which method describes the method of identifying vulnerabilities and threats and assessing the possible damage to determine where to implement security safeguards?
    A. Risk analysis
    B. Information management
    C. Countermeasure selection
    D. Classification controls

47. In CISSP exam asks the formula for total risk. What is the correct response?
    A. Annual Loss Expectancy (ALE) * Vulnerability = Total Risk
    B. Threat * Vulnerability * Asset Value (AV) = Total Risk
    C. Residual Risk (RR)/AV * Vulnerability = Total Risk
    D. AV/RR = Total Risk

48. What document gives detailed instructions about how to perform specific operations, providing a step-by-step guide?
    A. Policies
    B. Guidelines

C. Procedures

D. Standards

49. Which of the following can be used to keep availability?

A. Closed Circuit TV (CCTV)

B. Encryption

C. Checksums

D. Redundant array of inexpensive disks (RAID)

50. Which data classification method uses labels such as confidential, private, and sensitive?

A. Government

B. IP SEC

C. PUB SEC

D. Commercial

Chapter 2: Asset Security

1. Which of the following is not necessary for the data classification?

   A. Integrity
   B. Confidentiality
   C. Authority
   D. Availability

2. Which of the following role is not applicable for asset classification?

   A. User
   B. Officer
   C. Custodian
   D. Owner

3. Who provides practical protection of assets such as data?

   A. System Owner
   B. Data Owner
   C. Custodian
   D. Users

4. The entity that processes, stores, or transmits the information on behalf of the owner is called_____.

   A. Data processor
   B. Custodian
   C. Licensee
   D. Users

5. Data that remains after erasure or formatting the media is known as:

   A. Data Remanence
   B. Data classification

C. Residual data

D. Media sanitization

6. Which managerial role is accountable for the actual computers that house data, including the security of hardware and software configurations?

A. Custodian

B. Data owner

C. Mission owner

D. System owner

7. Which process ensured the data is not being damaged or corrupted?

A. Data destruction

B. Storage control

C. Maintenance

D. Usage instruction

8. _____ is done by way of formatting the media.

A. Data retention

B. Data Remanence

C. Data destruction

D. Data shredding

9. Which method does not helpful in protecting hardware data?

A. Encryption

B. Port protection

C. Storage control

D. Switching

10. _____ process help in password protection during the boot up process.

A. Port protection

B. BIOS checks

C. Encryption

D. Cable locks

11. The information in the minds of people, employees, managers, and other related individuals should also be secured. This statement related to?

    A. Data in media

    B. Data with personnel

    C. Data in hardware

    D. Data in software

12. Hard disk drives (HDDs), solid-state drives (SSDs), optical discs (CD/DVD) related to which states of data?

    A. Data in motion

    B. Data at rest

    C. Data in use

    D. None of the above

13. Internet is an example of _____ type of data.

    A. Data in motion

    B. Data at rest

    C. Data in use

    D. None of the above

14. Encryption, Secure Access Control and Segregation of duties are necessary for protection of _____ state.

    A. Data in use

    B. Data in motion

    C. Data at rest

    D. None of the above

15. The ISO/IEC 17799 standard was revised in 2005 and renumbered in 2007 as?

    A. BS 7799-1

    B. ISO 27000

    C. ISO 27001

    D. ISO 27002

16. Which control framework has 34 processes over four domains?

A. ISO
B. COBIT
C. ITIL®
D. OCTAVE®

17. Which phase of OCTAVE® conducts Risk Analysis and develops risk mitigation strategy?

A. Phase 1
B. Phase 2
C. Phase 3
D. Phase 4

18. Which procedure describes the process of determining which portions of a standard will be employed by an organization?

A. Baselines
B. Policies
C. Scoping
D. Tailoring

19. By which data protection method, integrity should be achieved?

A. Encryption
B. Cryptography
C. Hashing
D. Digital signatures

20. Which of the following describes a responsibility of the Data Owner?

A. Patch systems
B. Report suspicious activity
C. Ensure their files are backed up
D. Ensure data has proper security labels

21. As the data owner of the sales department, which is not the responsibility of the data owner?

A. Assigning information classifications
B. Dictating how data should be protected

C. Verifying the availability of data

D. Determining how long to retain the data

22. Assigning data classification levels can help with all of the following except:

A. Extracting data from a database

B. The combination of classified information with hierarchical and restrictive security

C. Ensuring that non sensitive data is not being protected by unnecessary controls

D. Lowering the costs of protecting data

23. The hiring manager has hired a new employee to fill a new post at Widgets, Inc.: Chief Privacy Officer (CPO). What is the primary function of her new role?

A. Ensuring the protection of partner data

B. Ensuring the security of customer, company, and employee data

C. Ensuring the accuracy and security of company financial information

D. Ensuring that security policies are defined and obligatory

24. As the participant of the data classification that does not determine, maintain or evaluate controls, so which role is that?

A. Data owner

B. Data custodian

C. Information systems auditor

D. Data user

25. Which of the following is NOT a factor determining the sensitivity of data?

A. Who should be accessing the data

B. The value of the data

C. The level of damage that could be affected should the data be exposed

D. How will the data be used?

26. When developing a data classification program in a company, what should be done first?

A. Understand the different levels of protection that must be provided

    B. Specify data classification criteria

    C. Identify the data custodians

    D. Determine protection mechanisms for each classification level

27. Which is the most valuable technique when determining if a specific security control should be applied?

    A. Cost/benefit analysis

    B. Risk analysis

    C. ALE results

    D. Identifying the vulnerabilities and threats producing the risk

28. What is the main security responsibility of a data owner?

    A. Determine how the data should be preserved

    B. Determine the data classification

    C. Determine the data value

    D. Determine how the data will be used

29. Which of the following is the initial stage in the life-cycle management of information?

    A. Data specification and classification

    B. Continuous monitoring and auditing of data access

    C. Data archival

    D. Database migration

30. Which of the following are effective methods of preventing data remanence on solid-state devices (SSDs)?

    A. Clearing

    B. Degaussing

    C. Purging

    D. Destruction

31. Which of the following are common military classes of data classification?

    A. Top secret, Secret, Classified, Unclassified

B. Top secret, Secret, Confidential, Private

C. Top secret, Secret, Confidential, Unclassified

D. Classified, Unclassified, Public

32. Which of the following method of data removal makes the data unrecoverable even with forensic effort?

A. Deletion of the data

B. Sanitization of the media

C. Purging via overwriting

D. None of these will work

33. When you're choosing the physical location for a new facility, which of the following should not avoid?

A. Hospitals

B. Airport flight paths

C. Chemical refineries

D. Railway freight lines

34. Which one of the following is not one of the three main sorts of fire-detection systems?

A. Heat sensing

B. Flame sensing

C. Carbon dioxide sensing

D. Smoke sensing

35. You are working as an incharge of a small area full of servers. Which of the following are the best protection against brownouts and temporary power loss?

A. UPS

B. RAID

C. Surge protectors

D. Voltage regulators

36. Which of the following relates to power degradation?

A. Blackouts

B. Spikes

C. Brownouts

D. Surge

37. What is a critical concern when discussing physical security?

    A. Guard dogs

    B. Layered access control

    C. Fences

    D. CCTV

38. What is one of the major drawbacks of using guard dogs as a physical security control?

    A. Legal liability

    B. Care

    C. Investment

    D. Training

39. What is a special type of identification means that does not require action by users because the user only needs to have it passed close to the ID device?

    A. Biometric systems

    B. Access control badges

    C. Proximity badges

    D. CCTV

40. What type of attack depends on the trusting nature of employees and the art of deception?

    A. Social engineering

    B. Hijacking

    C. Spoofing

    D. Deception

41. Which of the following reports about server rooms is incorrect?

A. Server rooms should have barriers on all six sides.

B. Server rooms should be kept at cold temperatures.

C. Server rooms should not be shared with IT workers.

D. Server rooms should be accessible to all IT staff.

42. What is the advantage of a contingency plan?

   A. Perimeter defense

   B. Diversity of controls

   C. Defense in layers

   D. Facility access controls

43. Which of the following lock types would rate as the most secure when installed properly?

   A. Wafer lock

   B. Cipher lock

   C. Combination lock

   D. Pin lock

44. When reviewing data security controls for data at rest, what is the least effective method to sanitize media such as hard drives?

   A. Formatting

   B. Drive wiping

   C. Degaussing

   D. Zeroization

45. Which of the following related to power loss?

   A. Brownouts

   B. Spikes and surges

   C. Blackouts

   D. Surges

46. During which phase/phases of the information life cycle can cryptography be an effective control?

   A. Use

   B. Archival

   C. Disposal

   D. All the above

47. Which of the following requirements addresses the data retention policy?

   A. Legal

   B. Regulatory

   C. Operational

   D. Maintenance

48. Who allows ultimate responsibility for the protection of assets within the organization?

   A. Data owners

   B. Cyber insurance providers

   C. Senior management

   D. Security professionals

49. What should be considered most when classifying data by the management?

   A. The type of employees, contractors, and customers who will be accessing the data

   B. Assessing the risk level and disabling countermeasures

   C. Confidentiality, Integrity, and Availability

   D. The access controls that will be protecting the data

50. A transition into the disposal phase of the information life cycle is most commonly generated by

   A. Data retention policies

   B. Senior management

   C. Insufficient storage

   D. Acceptable use policies

Chapter 3: Security Architecture & Engineering

1. Each TPM has a master wrapping key which is known as:
   A. Storage Root Key (SRK)
   B. Endorsement Key (EK)
   C. Attestation Identity Key (AIK)
   D. Storage Key

2. A public/private key pair that is installed in the TPM at the time of manufacture and cannot be modified is called:
   A. Storage Root Key (SRK)
   B. Endorsement Key (EK)
   C. Attestation Identity Key (AIK)
   D. Storage Key

3. TPM's internal memory is divided into _____ different segments:
   A. 2
   B. 4
   C. 6
   D. 8

4. What's the basic purpose of memory protection?
   A. Protects memory from being access by unauthorized programs.
   B. Prevents a program from being accessible to the memory used by another program.
   C. Protects memory from storing malicious codes.
   D. Protect memory from attacks.

5. Who generates a request to access the resources?
   A. Web server
   B. Proxy server
   C. Subject
   D. Object

6. Which server connects with the user to access the restricted sites?
   A. Web server
   B. Application server
   C. Proxy server
   D. Client server

7. Which of the following does not include in Asymmetric Key Algorithm?
   A. IDEA
   B. RSA
   C. DSA
   D. Elliptic Curve

8. How many types of access controls which can be implemented?
   A. 2
   B. 3
   C. 4
   D. 5

9. ISO/IEC 27001 assurance focuses on.
   A. Assurance focus on personal expertise and knowledge
   B. Assurance focus on security management
   C. Assurance focus on self-declaration
   D. Assurance focus on quality and development process

10. Which system covers all layers of protection and its integrated security mechanisms, control and concepts are reliable?
    A. Encrypted System
    B. Trusted System
    C. Password-Protected System
    D. Industrial Control System

11. Which model works with a multilevel security system?
    A. Biba
    B. Bell-LaPadula
    C. Clark-Wilson
    D. Graham-Denning

12. How many rules in Graham-Denning Model?

    A. 3

    B. 5

    C. 4

    D. 8

13. Which model also called the Chinese Wall Model?

    A. Graham-Denning Model

    B. Brewer and Nash Model

    C. Non-interference Model

    D. Clark-Wilson Model

14. Which security model addresses the integrity of data within a system?

    A. Biba

    B. Bell-LaPadula

    C. Clark-Wilson

    D. Graham-Denning

15. Which criteria is the formal implementation of the Bell-LaPadula model?

    A. Common Criteria

    B. TCSEC

    C. ITSEC

    D. All of the above

16. What type of rating is used within the Common Criteria framework?

    A. PP

    B. EPL

    C. EAL

    D. A–D

17. TPM chip was devised by?

    A. Common Criteria

    B. TCSEC

    C. ITSEC

    D. TCG

18. Sensitivity labels are a fundamental factor in which type of access control systems?

A. Mandatory access control
B. Discretionary access control
C. Access control lists
D. Role-based access control

19. The process of finding vulnerabilities in code, an encryption algorithm, or key management scheme is called _____
   A. Cryptographic
   B. Encryption
   C. Cryptanalysis
   D. Ciphering

20. Which technique gains information about cryptographic secret such as passwords, keys, encrypted files, by torturing a person?
   A. Adaptive Chosen Plaintext Attack
   B. Rubber Hose Attack
   C. Chosen Cipher-text Attack
   D. Known Plaintext Attack

21. Which device connects to the sensors that convert sensor data to digital data exclude telemetry hardware?
   A. PLCs
   B. RTUs
   C. Sensors
   D. Telemetry system

22. Which model offers a cloud-based infrastructure to deploy remote data center?
   A. IaaS
   B. IDaaS
   C. PaaS
   D. SaaS

23. Which clouds are accessed by multiple parties having common goals and shared resources?
   A. Private
   B. Hybrid
   C. Community

D. public

24. What does DES stand for?
    A. Data Encryption System
    B. Data Encryption Standard
    C. Data Encoding Standard
    D. Data Encryption Signature

25. Which of the following uses a symmetric key and hashing algorithm?
    A. HMAC
    B. Triple-DES
    C. EAS
    D. RSA

26. DES performs how many rounds of transposition/permutation and substitution?
    A. 16
    B. 32
    C. 64
    D. 56

27. Which of the following best defines a digital signature?
    A. A method of transferring a handwritten signature to an electronic document
    B. A method to encrypt confidential information
    C. A method to provide an electronic signature and encryption
    D. A method to let the receiver of the message prove the source and integrity of a message

28. Which of the following is based on the fact that it is difficult to factor large numbers into two original prime numbers?
    A. ECC
    B. RSA
    C. DES
    D. Diffie-Hellman

29. A 160-bit EC key is equivalent to _____bit RSA key.
    A. 64

B. 1024

C. 32

D. 256

30. Which of the following is true about the digital signatures?
A. The sender generates the hash of plaintext through a public key
B. The sender encrypts the hash through a private key
C. The sender encrypts the plaintext through a public key
D. The sender encrypts the plaintext through a private key

31. EMI issues such as crosstalk primarily influence which aspect of security?
A. Confidentiality
B. Availability
C. Integrity
D. Authentication

32. Which security architecture model defines the way to develop access rights between subjects and objects securely?
A. Brewer-Nash
B. Clark-Wilson
C. Bell-LaPadula
D. Graham-Denning

33. Which of the following best describes the type of protection that needs to be delivered by this product?
A. Data Execution Prevention
B. Hardware isolation
C. Memory induction application
D. Domain isolation protection

34. Which of the following arises in a PKI environment?
A. The RA creates the certificate, and the CA signs it.
B. The RA signs the certificate.
C. The CA signs the certificate.
D. The user signs the certificate.

35. Which of the following properly describes the difference between public key cryptography and public key infrastructure?
    A. Public key cryptography is the use of an asymmetric algorithm, while the public key
    infrastructure is the use of a symmetric algorithm.
    B. Public key cryptography is another name of asymmetric cryptography, while public key infrastructure consists of public key cryptographic mechanisms.
    C. Public key cryptography is used to generate public/private key pairs, and public key
    infrastructure is used to perform key exchange and agreement.
    D. Public key cryptography offers authentication and non-repudiation, while public key infrastructure provides confidentiality and integrity.

36. Which of the following best defines Key Derivation Functions (KDFs)?
    A. Session keys are generated from each other.
    B. Asymmetric cryptography is used to encrypt symmetric keys.
    C. Keys are generated from a master key.
    D. A master key is generated from a session key.

37. An elliptic curve cryptosystem is an asymmetric algorithm. What makes different from other asymmetric algorithms?
    A. It provides digital signatures, secure key distribution, and encryption.
    B. It computes discrete logarithms in a finite field.
    C. It uses a larger percentage of resources to carry out encryption.
    D. It is more efficient.

38. Which of the following working similarly to stream ciphers?
    A. One-time pad
    B. AES
    C. Block
    D. RSA

39. In cryptography, different methods and algorithms provide different types of security services. Which of the following provides only authentication, non-repudiation, and integrity?
    A. Encryption algorithm
    B. Digital signature

C. Hash algorithm

D. Encryption paired with a digital signature

40. AES is an algorithm used for which of the following?

A. Data integrity

B. Bulk data encryption

C. Key recovery

D. Distribution of symmetric keys

41. How many keys must be generated for the 260 employees using the company's PKI asymmetric algorithm?

A. 33,670

B. 520

C. 67,340

D. 260

42. What are the address requirements of the Take-Grant model?

A. Confidentiality

B. Integrity

C. Authentication

D. Availability

43. When discussing security evaluation models, what is the name of the TCSEC A1 specification?

A. Labeled security protection

B. Structured protection

C. Security domains

D. Verified design

44. Which of the following is a condition for the TCSEC B2 specification?

A. Trusted path requirements

B. Protection from covert channels

C. First level to require sensitivity labels

D. Configuration management procedures must be enforced

45. Common Criteria (CC)defines which of the following?

A. A target of the review

B. Rainbow series requirements

C. Seven assurance levels

D. Ten functionality classes and seven evaluation levels

46. Which EAL level could be described as formally verified, designed, and tested?

A. EAL 2

B. EAL 4

C. EAL 6

D. EAL 7

47. Which European standard addresses confidentiality, integrity, and availability?

A. Trusted Computer System Evaluation Criteria (TCSEC)

B. Information Technology Security Evaluation Criteria (ITSEC)

C. Common Criteria (CC)

D. ISO 17799

48. Which model is primarily concerned with conflicts of interest?

A. Bell-LaPadula

B. Sutherland

C. Brewer and Nash

D. Biba

49. What process usually takes place after generating a DES session key?

A. Key exchange

B. Key signing

C. Key escrow

D. Key clustering

50. What would indicate that a message had been changed?

A. The public key has been altered.

B. The message digest has been altered.

C. The private key has been altered.

D. The message has been encrypted properly.

Chapter 4: Communication & Network Security

1. What are the arrangements of the OSI reference model layer from bottom to top?
   A. Physical, Data Link, Transport, Network, Session, Presentation, Application
   B. Physical, Network, Data Link, Transport, Session, Presentation, Application
   C. Physical, Data Link, Network, Transport, Session, Presentation, Application
   D. Physical, Data Link, Network, Transport, Presentation, Session, Application

2. In which layer of the OSI model adds the source and destination Media Access Control (MAC) address to the frame?
   A. Session Layer
   B. Data Link Layer
   C. Transport Layer
   D. Physical Layer

3. How many bits represent the Organization Unique Identifier (OUI) in MAC addresses?
   A. 48-bits
   B. 32-bits
   C. 16-bits
   D. 24-bits

4. From the following protocols, Transport layer does not belong.
   A. Simple Key Management for Internet Protocols (SKIP)
   B. Sequenced Packet Exchange (SPX)
   C. Secure Sockets Layer (SSL)
   D. Transport Layer Security (TLS)

5. Which networking device operates at the Application layer (Layer 7)?
   A. B-router
   B. Bridge

    C. Gateway

    D. Hub

6. Which layer of the TCP/IP model corresponds to the Physical and Data-Link Layer of the OSI model?

    A. Transport

    B. Link

    C. Internet

    D. Application

7. In IP class, how many hosts supported by a full class B subnet?

    A. 254

    B. 0

    C. 65,534

    D. 16,777,214

8. Which of the following statement does not describe the benefit of Multilayer Protocol?

    A. A wide range of protocols can be used at higher layers.

    B. Covert channels are allowed.

    C. Encryption can be integrated at various layers.

    D. Supports Flexibility and resiliency in complex network structures.

9. Which mechanism is designed to handle a wide range of protocols through encapsulation?

    A. MPLS

    B. Converged protocols

    C. Multilayer protocols

    D. VoIP

10. Which common VoIP protocol designed to carry streaming audio and video?

    A. SIP

    B. H.323

    C. RPC

D. RTP

11. Secure Real-time Transport Protocol uses_____ for confidentiality.
    A. CHAP
    B. AES
    C. PAP
    D. RADIUS

12. WEP uses an RC4 stream cipher to achieve _____.
    A. Integrity
    B. Confidentiality
    C. Authentication
    D. Encryption

13. Which security protocol uses WPA to address the encryption problems in WEP.
    A. EAP
    B. OSA
    C. TKIP
    D. SKA

14. Which authentication method uses a four-way handshake to authenticate.
    A. Shared Key Authentication
    B. Open System Authentication
    C. Temporal Key Integrity Protocol
    D. Extensible Authentication Protocol

15. Which of the following protocols perform in the following layers: application, data link, network, and transport?
    A. FTP, ARP, TCP, and UDP
    B. FTP, ICMP, IP, and UDP
    C. TFTP, ARP, IP, and UDP
    D. TFTP, RARP, IP, and ICMP

16. Virtual Network Computing (VNC) and Remote Desktop Protocol (RDP), are common modern protocols used in _____.
    A. Desktop and Application Virtualization
    B. Screen Scraping
    C. Virtual private networks
    D. Remote Desktop Console Access

17. Which network uses a series of distributed caching servers to improve performance and lower the latency of downloaded online content?
    A. Software Defined Network
    B. Content Distribution Network
    C. Virtual Private Network
    D. Remote Based Network

18. Which of the following proxies make decisions based upon a single packet?
    A. Application
    B. Packet filtering
    C. Circuit
    D. Stateful

19. Which of the following is the best sort of fiber for long distance communication?
    A. Single mode
    B. Multimode
    C. Optical carrier
    D. SONET

20. What is the most secure type of EAP?
    A. EAP-TLS
    B. EAP-TTLS
    C. LEAP
    D. PEAP

21. Accessing an IPv6 network via an IPv4 network is called what?
    A. CIDR

B. Tunneling
C. Translation
D. NAT

22. What is the most secure type of firewall?
    A. Application-layer proxy firewall
    B. Stateful firewall
    C. Circuit-level proxy firewall
    D. Packet filter

23. Restricting Bluetooth device discovery relies on which basis?
    A. Symmetric key
    B. MAC address
    C. Private key
    D. Public key

24. Layer 2 of the OSI model has two sublayers. What are those sublayers?
    A. LCL and MAC
    B. LCL and MCA
    C. Network and MAC
    D. LLC and MAC

25. What are two IEEE standards that label technologies at layer 2?
    A. IEEE 802.1 and 802.2
    B. IEEE 802.2 and 802.3
    C. IEEE 801.1 and 801.2
    D. IEEE 803.1 and 803.2

26. Which of the following would be best to practice as a VPN tunneling solution?
    A. PPTP
    B. L2P
    C. IPSec
    D. L2TP

27. Which of the following correctly describes Bluejacking?
    A. Bluejacking is a harmful, malicious attack.
    B. It is usually used to send unsolicited messages.
    C. It is the process of taking over another portable device by a Bluetooth-enabled device.
    D. The term was created by the use of a Bluetooth device and the act of hijacking another device.

28. Which of the following is a proprietary interior protocol that selects the best path between the source and destination?
    A. BGP
    B. RIP
    C. IGRP
    D. OSPF

29. Which of the following does NOT define IP telephony security?
    A. VoIP networks should be protected with the same security controls used on a data
    network.
    B. Softphones are more secure than IP phones.
    C. As endpoints, IP phones can become the target of attacks.
    D. The current Internet design over which voice is transmitted is less secure than physical phone lines.

30. Which of the following is not an advantage of VoIP?
    A. Security
    B. Convergence
    C. Flexibility
    D. Cost

31. What type of security encryption component use WEP?
    A. Service Set ID
    B. Temporal Key Integrity Protocol
    C. Ad hoc WLAN
    D. Open system authentication

32. _____ is a set of extensions to DNS that provides to DNS clients origin authentication of DNS data to reduce the threat of DNS.
    A. Resource records
    B. Zone transfer
    C. DNSSEC
    D. Resource transfer

33. Which technology determines the terrestrial location of a client IP address to route it toward the most proximal topological source of web content?
    A. Content domain distribution (CDD)
    B. Distributed name service (DNS)
    C. Distributed web service (DWS)
    D. Content distribution network (CDN)

34. Which of the following protocols is used in Voice over IP (VoIP) for caller identification?
    A. Real-time Transport Protocol (RTP)
    B. Real-time Transport Control Protocol (RTCP)
    C. Session Initiation Protocol (SIP)
    D. Phone Branch Exchange (PBX)

35. Where does PPTP encryption take place in OSI model?
    A. Network layer
    B. Data link layer
    C. Transport layer
    D. Data link and physical layers

36. Which of the following protocols blurs the outlines between the OSI model layers, performing the tasks of several at once?
    A. Transmission Control Protocol (TCP)
    B. File Transfer Protocol (FTP)
    C. Distributed Network Protocol 3 (DNP3)
    D. Domain Name System (DNS)

37. Which of the following properly describes the relationship between SSL and TLS?
    A. SSL can be modified by developers to increase the protocol's capabilities.
    B. TLS is a proprietary protocol, while SSL is an open-community protocol.
    C. SSL is more extensible and backward compatible with TLS.
    D. TLS is the open-community version of SSL.

38. Which of the following INACCURATELY labels IP spoofing and session hijacking?
    A. Address spoofing helps an attacker to hijack sessions between two users without being detected.
    B. IP spoofing is used to hijack SSL and IPSec secure communications.
    C. IP spoofing makes it harder to track down an attacker.
    D. Session hijacking can be prevented with common authentication.

39. Which of the following best describes why e-mail spoofing is effortlessly affected?
    A. Keyword filtering is technically obsolete.
    B. Administrators often forget to configure an SMTP server to avoid inbound SMTP connections for domains it doesn't serve.
    C. SMTP lacks an adequate authentication mechanism.
    D. Blacklists are undependable.

40. Which of the following are the accurate specifications for 802.11g?
    A. 5 GHz and 11 Mbps

B. 2.4 GHz and 54 Mbps
C. 5 GHz and 54 Mbps
D. 2.4 GHz and 54 Mbps

41. LAN data transmissions can take on several different methods. Which of the following can be both a source and a destination address?
A. Anycast
B. Multicast
C. Broadcast
D. Unicast

42. Which data transmission associated with IPv6?
A. Anycast
B. Multicast
C. Broadcast
D. Unicast

43. Which network device operates at the internetworking layer of the TCP/IP model?
A. Router
B. Firewall
C. PBX
D. Switch

44. From a security perspective, what is the most common complaint about email?
A. Plain-text passwords
B. Spam
C. Incompatible mail programs
D. Weak authentication

45. Which of the following is the less secure communications protocol?
A. CHAP
B. IPsec
C. PAP
D. EAP

46. Which of the following solutions is best to describe the company's need to protect wireless traffic?
A. EAP-TLS
B. EAP-PEAP
C. LEAP
D. EAP-TTLS

47. Which of the following is the best solution to meet the company's need for broadband wireless connectivity?
    A. IEEE 802.16
    B. IEEE 802.12
    C. WPA2
    D. IEEE 802.15

48. Which of the following proxies cannot decide access decisions based upon protocol commands?
    A. Circuit
    B. Application
    C. Packet filtering
    D. Stateful

49. Which is an effective method to shield networks from unauthenticated DHCP clients?
    A. DHCP protection
    B. DHCP snooping
    C. DHCP shielding
    D. DHCP caching

50. Signaling protocol that is widely used for controlling multimedia communication sessions such as voice and video calls over IP is?
    A. SS7
    B. Real-time Transport Protocol
    C. SIP
    D. VoIP

Chapter 5: Identity & Access Management (IAM)

1. Which of the following would not be an asset that an organization would want to protect with access controls?
   A. Information
   B. Systems
   C. Devices
   D. Facilities
   E. None of the above

2. Which access control implies all authorization verification is done by a single entity?
   A. Decentralized Access Control
   B. Centralized Access Control
   C. Role Based Access Control
   D. Rule Based Access Control

3. Which of the following provides authentication based on a physical characteristic of a subject?
   A. Account ID
   B. Biometrics
   C. Token
   D. PIN

4. Which of the following is an example of a Type 2 authentication factor?
   A. Something you have
   B. Something you are
   C. Something you do
   D. Something you know

5. Which is the ability to track user's actions as they access systems and data?
   A. Auditing
   B. Authentication

C. Accountability

D. Authorization

6. _____ can be used in LDAP directory for dynamic authentication systems.
   A. Subdata
   B. Predata
   C. Metadata
   D. Prodata

7. Lightweight Directory Access Protocol (LDAP) uses _____ for authentication purpose.
   A. Kerberos
   B. PAP
   C. CHAP
   D. EAP

8. Which system can be used to prevent the authentication system from unauthorized access?
   A. Registration
   B. Identification
   C. Proofing
   D. Session managing

9. SAML and SPML often used in _____ system.
   A. Federated Identity management
   B. Credential management
   C. Session management
   D. Asset management

10. Administration makes credentials secure by?
    A. Ciphering
    B. Cryptography
    C. Encrypting
    D. Steganography

11. Which model describes how the subject can access objects?
    A. OSI

B. TCP/IP

C. Access control

D. None of above

12. What type of access control Role-based Access Control(RBAC) belongs to?
   A. Discretionary
   B. Nondiscretionary
   C. Mandatory
   D. Centralized

13. Which access control system is based on if/then statement?
   A. Rule-based
   B. Attribute-based
   C. Role-based
   D. Mandatory

14. _____ access control based on a subject's clearance and an object's labels.
   A. RBAC
   B. DAC
   C. ABAC
   D. MAC

15. Which model is implemented using ACLs?
   A. RBAC
   B. DAC
   C. ABAC
   D. MAC

16. _____ is an advanced implementation of a Rule-BAC model.
   A. RBAC
   B. DAC
   C. ABAC
   D. MAC

17. In discretionary access control security, who has delegation authority to grant access to data?
   A. User

B. Security officer

C. Security policy

D. Owner

18. What role does biometrics show in access control?

A. Authorization

B. Authentication

C. Accountability

D. None of the above

19. Which act is responsible for removal or disable user account when he leaves the organization?

A. Enrolment

B. De-provisioning

C. Provisioning

D. Reporting

20. Which access control method is considered user-directed?

A. Nondiscretionary

B. Mandatory

C. Identity-based

D. Discretionary

21. What service is known as cloud identity, which allows organizations to influence cloud service for identity management?

A. IaaS

B. SaaS

C. PaaS

D. IDaaS

22. What access control method weighs additional factors, the control uses the content?

A. Content-dependent access control

B. Context-dependent access control

C. Role-based access control

D. Task-based access control

23. What access control method considers additional factors, such as time of attempted access, before granting access?
   A. Role-based access control
   B. Task-based access control
   C. Context-dependent access control
   D. Content-dependent access control

24. What is an XML-based structure for exchanging security information, including third-party authentication?
   A. Kerberos
   B. OpenID
   C. SAML
   D. SESAME

25. Which of the following is not XML-based exchanging security information?
   A. Kerberos
   B. OpenID
   C. SAML
   D. SESAME

26. Which of the following is the only open protocol for interfacing and querying directory service information?
   A. CHAP
   B. PAP
   C. LDAP
   D. RADIUS

27. What Markup language representing data structures but not sharing security information?
   A. XML
   B. SPML
   C. XACML
   D. GML

28. What Markup language created by IBM for formatting documents?
   A. XML
   B. SPML

> **C.** XACML
> **D.** GML

29. What Markup language allows for the sharing of application security policies to ensure the same security rules?
    A. XML
    B. SPML
    C. XACML
    D. GML

30. Of the following, what is the primary point that bound ACL is based upon?
    A. A subject
    B. An object
    C. A product
    D. An application

31. Of the following, what is the primary point that a capability table is based upon?
    A. A subject
    B. An object
    C. A product
    D. An application

32. Investigations are a good example of which of the following?
    A. Detective control
    B. Preventive control
    C. Deterrent control
    D. Proactive control

33. Which of the following is the best example of capabilities tables?
    A. Memory cards
    B. Kerberos
    C. Constrained user interface
    D. Router ACL

34. Which form of access control has a many-to-many relationship and makes use of mapping between a user and a subset of goals?
    A. MAC

B. DAC
C. Rule-based access control
D. RBAC

35. Which of the following mentions to the process of creation, maintenance, and deletion of user objects?
A. Identification
B. Verification
C. Authentication
D. Provisioning

36. Which attack using the established personal information to gain access to accounts, cell phone records, or other information?
A. Pretexting
B. Social engineering
C. Dumpster diving
D. Phishing

37. What nontechnical attack attempts to lure the prey into giving up financial data, credit card numbers, or other types of account information?
A. Pretexting
B. Social engineering
C. Dumpster diving
D. Phishing

38. Key Distribution Center is a component of what?
A. TACACS
B. Kerberos
C. RADIUS
D. SESAME

39. The Privilege Attribute Certificate (PAC) belongs to?
A. TACACS
B. Kerberos
C. RADIUS
D. SESAME

40. The ticket-granting service is a factor of what?
   A. TACACS
   B. RADIUS
   C. Kerberos
   D. SESAME

41. Which of the following are the most luxurious means of verifying a user's identity?
   A. Single sign-on
   B. Tokens
   C. Biometrics
   D. Passwords

42. What method of authorization is closely associated with labels?
   A. Rule-based access control
   B. Discretionary access control
   C. Mandatory access control
   D. Role-based access control

43. Access Control List (ACL) includes which of the following?
   A. Role- and task-based
   B. Rule-based and mandatory
   C. Labeled and mandatory
   D. None of the above

44. What type of physical control removes inappropriate actions?
   A. Deterrent
   B. Detective
   C. Preventive
   D. Corrective

45. What sort of physical control is a mantrap?
   A. Deterrent
   B. Corrective
   C. Preventive
   D. Detective

46. What is an example of passive attack?

A. Dumpster diving

B. Sniffing

C. Installing SubSeven

D. Social engineering

47. Which biometric authentication system is maximum associated with law enforcement?

A. Fingerprint recognition

B. Iris recognition

C. Facial recognition

D. Retina pattern recognition

48. Which of the following is the most time-intensive sort of offline password attack to attempt?

A. Hybrid

B. Plain text

C. Brute-force

D. Man-in-the-middle

49. Which of the following is not one of the three primary types of authentication?

A. Something you remember

B. Something you know

C. Something you are

D. Something you have

50. Which could be considered a single point of failure within a single sign-on application?

A. Authentication server

B. User's workstation

C. Logon credentials

D. RADIUS

Chapter 6: Security Assessment & Testing

1. All of the following are steps in the security audit process except which one?
   A. Determination of goals & scope
   B. Conduct an Audit
   C. Convene a management review
   D. Documentation

2. In which assessment strategy should align with the organization's business and day-to-day operations.
   A. Internal
   B. External
   C. Third-party
   D. Both B and C

3. Which strategy should complement the internal strategy to ensure the organization meets its compliance goals?
   A. Internal
   B. External
   C. Third-party
   D. Both B and C

4. An assessment whose goal is to assess the susceptibility of an organization to social engineering attacks is best categorized as
   A. Physical testing
   B. Network testing
   C. Personnel testing
   D. Vulnerability testing

5. The goal of _____ is to identify elements in an environment that are not effectively protected.
   A. Physical testing

    B. Network testing

    C. Personnel testing

    D. Vulnerability testing

6. What type of assessment would best exhibit an organizations' compliance with PCI-DSS?

    A. Audit

    B. Penetration test

    C. Security assessment

    D. Vulnerability assessment

7. The main goal of Penetration testing is

    A. Identify risk

    B. Mitigate risk

    C. Acceptance risk

    D. Assignment risk

8. Penetration testing goes through the following steps except one:

    A. Discovery

    B. Enumeration

    C. Exploitation

    D. Vulnerability scanning

9. A log is a _____ type of data.

    A. Write Once Read Many (WORM)

    B. Write Many Read Once (WMRO)

    C. Write Once Read Once (WORO)

    D. Write Many Read Many (WMRM)

10. What can be run on a periodic basis to ensure the application meets the performing requirement?

    A. Integration testing

    B. Installation testing

    C. Synthetic transaction

D. Unit testing

11. _____ is the foundation of software assessment programs.
   A. Code review
   B. Test coverage analysis
   C. Interface testing
   D. Misuse case testing

12. Testing the additional purpose of system and software has been done by
   A. Code review
   B. Test coverage analysis
   C. Interface testing
   D. Misuse case testing

13. Which type of testing has no prior knowledge of the testing environment?
   A. White box testing
   B. Black box testing
   C. Grey box testing
   D. Static testing

14. What type of testing environment ensure complete code coverage?
   A. White box
   B. Grey box
   C. Black box
   D. Dynamic

15. Account management is responsible for the following except
   A. Modifying accounts
   B. Managing accounts
   C. Creating accounts
   D. Securing accounts

16. What information security management task ensures that the organization's data protection requirements are met effectively?
    A. Account management
    B. Backup verification
    C. Log review
    D. Key performance indicators

17. Reports are focused on service organization's systems including a report about the suitability of the control operating effectively to meet its objective, is described in which type of reporting?
    A. SOC 1 Type 1
    B. SOC 2
    C. SOC 1 Type 2
    D. SOC 3

18. You are working with your company to validate assessment and audit strategies. The immediate goal is to ensure that all auditors are following the processes and procedures defined by the company's audit policies. Which type of audit should you use for this scenario?
    A. Internal
    B. External
    C. Third-party
    D. Hybrid

19. Choose the term that describes an audit report that covers the information security controls of a service organization and is intended for public release.
    A. SOC 1
    B. SOC 2
    C. SOC 3
    D. Both B and C.

20. What is the difference between security training and security awareness training?
    A. Security training is focused on skills, while security awareness training is focused on recognizing and responding to issues.

    B. Security training must be performed, while security awareness training is an aspirational goal.

    C. Security awareness training is focused on security personnel, while security training is geared toward all users.

    D. There is no difference. These terms refer to the same process.

21. What can be used to examines multiple software components as they are combined into a working system?

    A. Integration testing

    B. Installation testing

    C. Acceptance testing

    D. Unit testing

22. What can be used to ensure that software meets the customer's operational requirements?

    A. Integration testing

    B. Installation testing

    C. Acceptance testing

    D. Unit testing

23. What type of testing method does not require access to source code?

    A. Secure compiler warnings

    B. Fuzzing

    C. Static testing

    D. White-box testing

24. Which of the following describes a full-interruption test during disaster recovery testing?

    A. It is performed to ensure that critical systems will run at the different site.

B. All departments receive a copy of the recovery plan to review it for completeness.

C. Agents from each department come together and go through the test collectively.

D. Normal operations are shut down.

25. Which of the following defines a structured walk-through test during disaster recovery testing?

   A. It is performed to ensure that critical systems will run at the alternative site.

   B. All departments receive a copy of the recovery plan to review it for completeness.

   C. Agents from each department come together and go through the test collectively.

   D. Normal operations are shut down.

26. What are the main stages of account management?

   A. Provisioning or adding accounts, modifying accounts, and suspending accounts

   B. Adding accounts, deleting accounts, and deleting users' data

   C. Verifying account passwords, validating account usage, and deleting accounts

   D. Provisioning accounts, modifying accounts, auditing the use of accounts, and suspending accounts

27. What are the key stages of authentication management?

   A. Provisioning or adding accounts, modifying accounts, and suspending accounts

   B. Adding accounts, deleting accounts, and deleting users' data

   C. Verifying account passwords, validating account usage, and deleting accounts

   D. Provisioning accounts, modifying accounts, auditing the use of accounts, and suspending accounts.

28. What is a code review?

    A. Making sure coders work in parallel to watch each other's work while they are coding

    B. Making sure coders' work has been reviewed by other coders after they are done

    C. Making sure that the appropriate Q/A harnesses have been applied before check-in

    D. Making sure that appropriate Q/A harnesses exist

29. Which of the following is the most significant reason to log events remotely?

    A. To prevent against log tampering

    B. To have several copies of the logs of every event

    C. To make it easier to back up the logs on a single write-once media

    D. To facilitate log review and analysis

30. When providing a security report to management, which of the following is the main element?

    A. A list of threats, vulnerabilities, and the probabilities that they will occur

    B. A comprehensive list of the probabilities and impacts of adverse events anticipated

    C. An executive summary that is comprehensive but does not exceed two pages

    D. An executive summary that is as long as is necessary to be technically comprehensive

31. Why are security metrics so vital as performance and risk indicators?

    A. They can be used to document deviations from standards.

    B. They enable management to understand the performance of a security program.

C. They can help auditors determine whether incidents have been properly resolved.

D. They can be used to determine the cost of a countermeasure.

32. What is a synthetic transaction?

A. A bogus user transaction that must be disallowed

B. User behavior intended to falsify records

C. A scripted process used to emulate user behavior

D. A scripted process by an attacker used to violate policy

33. How can a backup strategy be prepared most effective?

A. By ensuring that all user data is backed up

B. By testing restoration procedures

C. By backing up database management systems (DBMSs) via their proprietary methods

D. By reviewing backup logs to ensure they are complete

34. Which of the following defines a parallel test during disaster recovery testing?

A. It is performed to ensure that some systems will run at the alternative site.

B. All departments receive a copy of the disaster recovery plan to review it for completeness.

C. Agents from each department come together and go through the test c collectively.

D. Normal operations are shut down.

35. When is a team investigating a potential network intrusion, which of the following would be the best way for team members to communicate?

A. Email

   B. VoIP phones

   C. Instant Messenger

   D. Cell phone

36. What is Tripwire used for?

   A. Tripwire is a host-based IDS.

   B. Tripwire is a file integrity monitoring tool.

   C. Tripwire is a network-based IDS.

   D. Tripwire is a signature-based IDS.

37. What is the name of the software that inhibits users from seeing all items or directories on a computer and changes process output?

   A. Hidden file attributes

   B. File obscurity

   C. NTFS data streams

   D. Root kit

38. Chain of custody comprises which of the following?

   A. Who, what, where, when, and how

   B. Who, when, why, how, motive, and where

   C. What, why, and how

   D. What, when, and where

39. What is criminal activity directly directed against network devices called?

   A. Criminal violations

   B. Civil violations

   C. Computer crime

    D. Illegal penetration testing

40. Which of the following is measured a commercial application of steganography?

    A. Hashing

    B. Data diddling

    C. Digital watermarks

    D. XOR encryption

41. Entrapment is best defined by which of the following statements?

    A. It is illegal.

    B. It is legal.

    C. It is neither legal nor ethical.

    D. It is legal with a court order or warrant.

42. Enticement is best defined by which of the following statements?

    A. It is illegal.

    B. It is legal.

    C. It is neither legal nor ethical.

    D. It is legal with a court order or warrant.

43. Senior management wanted to protect the company from network attacks or security breaches. What is this type of behavior called?

    A. Due diligence

    B. Due care

    C. Risk negligence

    D. Due prudence

44. Facility monitoring through the use of CCTV is an example of which of the following?

   A. Enticement

   B. Computer surveillance

   C. Entrapment

   D. Physical surveillance

45. What kind of evidence provided as an oral or written statement?

   A. Secondary evidence

   B. Real evidence

   C. Direct evidence

   D. Demonstrative evidence

46. Which of the following is the key reason for the chain of custody?

   A. To prevent the defense from challenging

   B. To demonstrate evidence was properly controlled and handled

   C. To verify whether the copy that was used is admissible

   D. To verify changes to data

47. Which of the following is not a form of social engineering?

   A. Pretexting

   B. Fishing

   C. Whaling

   D. Blackmailing

48. Which test adherence to the user accounts policy?

   A. User self-reporting

B. Penetration testing

C. Management review

D. User records auditing

49. All of the following are types of tests for disaster recovery and business continuity plans except which one?

   A. Structured walk-through test

   B. Simulation test

   C. Null hypothesis test

   D. Full-interruption test

50. Who is responsible for PCI-DSS standards?

   A. ISO

   B. EU

   C. U.S. Government

   D. Major credit-card companies

Chapter 7: Security Operations

1. Which deals with collecting, preserving, and producing the evidence that pertains to computer crimes?
    A. Digital investigations
    B. Digital forensics
    C. Both A and B
    D. Documentation

2. The reporting phase of the incident handling begins immediately with _____.
    A. Recovery
    B. Detection
    C. Retention
    D. Documentation

3. Non-technical reporting is responsible for notifying about any serious incidents and the latest incident handling updates to.
    A. Stakeholders
    B. Custodian
    C. Security personnel
    D. Customers

4. After reporting, what will be the next step in incident handling?
    A. Recovery
    B. Detection
    C. Retention
    D. Documentation

5. Which tool used in the forensic world for evidence collection?
    A. Forensic Toolkit (FTK)
    B. EnCase forensic

C. File copy tool

D. dd Unix utility

6. SEC and FINRA belong to which part of the investigation type?
   A. Civil
   B. Criminal
   C. Administrative
   D. Regulatory

7. Which system can detect anomalous activity on a network by using various methods?
   A. NIDS
   B. NIPS
   C. HIPS
   D. HIDS

8. Correlation of security-related data across dissimilar source is the primary utility provided by _____.
   A. Egress monitoring
   B. SIEM
   C. Continuous monitoring
   D. DLP

9. Which provisioning resources helps organizations to protect physical assets from theft, maintain software licensing compliance, and accounts?
   A. Asset management
   B. Configuration management
   C. Asset inventory
   D. Change management

10. Which of the following is an essential characteristic of evidence for it to be admissible?
    A. It must be real
    B. It must be noteworthy

C. It must be reliable

D. It must be important

11. What is the key difference between least privilege and need to know?

A. A user should have least privilege that limits need to know

B. A user should have a security clearance to access resources, a need to know about those resources, and least privilege to give full control of all resources

C. A user should need to know to access particular resources, and least privilege should be implemented to ensure only accesses the resources need to know.

D. They are two different terms for the same issue

12. What is the main benefit of job rotation and separation of duties policies?

A. Preventing collusion

B. Preventing fraud

C. Encouraging collusion

D. Correcting incidents

13. Which one of the following security tools is not proficient at generating an active response to a security event?

A. IPS

B. Firewall

C. IDS

D. Antivirus software

14. From an operations-security perspective, which of the following is one of the key areas when dealing with software?

A. Enabling local administrator rights

B. Software licensing

C. Enabling automatic updates

D. Changing time zones

15. How many phases of the incident management process?

A. 4

B. 5

C. 7

D. 3

16. Which technique can application developers use to test applications in an isolated virtualized environment before allowing them on a production network?
   A. Penetration testing
   B. Sandboxing
   C. White box testing
   D. Black box testing

17. Which property of a system recovers quickly after an incident happens?
   A. Resilience
   B. QoS
   C. Fault tolerance
   D. High availability

18. Which of the following is not a measure of a patch management process?
   A. Report patches
   B. Distribute patches
   C. Deploy all patches
   D. Detection of new patches

19. What would an administrator practice to check systems for known issues that attackers may use to exploit the systems?
   A. Port scanner
   B. Vulnerability scanner
   C. Security audit
   D. Security review

20. In which disaster recovery plan, teams must go through their documented recovery plans?
   A. Parallel
   B. Tabletop
   C. Read-through

D. Simulation

21. Which level of RAID does NOT offer additional reliability?

A. RAID 1

B. RAID 0

C. RAID 5

D. RAID 3

22. Maximum Tolerable Downtime (MTD) is consist of which two metrics?

A. Recovery Time Objective (RPO) and Work Recovery Time (WRT)

B. Recovery Point Objective (RPO) and Mean Time to Repair (MTTR)

C. Recovery Point Objective (RTO) and Work Recovery Time (WRT)

D. Recovery Time Objective (RTO) and Mean Time to Repair (MTTR)

23. Which plan details the steps required to take long term business operations after recovering from a disruptive event?

A. Business Continuity Plan (BCP)

B. Business Resumption Plan (BRP)

C. Continuity of Operations Plan (COOP)

D. Occupant Emergency Plan (OEP)

24. What metric defines how long it will take to recover data and made available for users?

A. Minimum Operating Requirements (MOR)

B. Mean Time Between Failures (MTBF)

C. The Mean Time to Repair (MTTR)

D. Recovery Point Objective (RPO)

25. What metric designates how long it will take to recover a failed system?

    A. Minimum Operating Requirements (MOR)

    B. Mean Time Between Failures (MTBF)

    C. The Mean Time to Repair (MTTR)

    D. Recovery Point Objective (RPO)

26. _____ offers fault tolerance for hard drives and can improve system performance.

    A. Disc duping

    B. Clustering

    C. RAID

    D. Virtualization

27. _____ offers for availability and scalability. It groups physically different systems and combines them logically, which helps to provide immunity to faults and improves performance.

    A. Disc duping

    B. Clustering

    C. RAID

    D. Virtualization

28. The operation does not necessarily mean that it backs up all the files that have been modified since the last time a backup process was run?

    A. Incremental process

    B. Full backup

    C. Partial backup

    D. Differential process

29. Which type of backup process backs up files that have been altered since the last time all data was backed up?

   A. Incremental process

   B. Full backup

   C. Partial backup

   D. Differential process

30. Which of the following steps happens first in a damage assessment? A damage assessment needs to take place after a disaster occurs.

   A. Determine the source of the disaster.

   B. Identify the resources that must be replaced immediately.

   C. Declare a disaster.

   D. Determine how long it will take to bring critical functions back online.

31. Which of the following steps happens last in a damage assessment? A damage assessment needs to take place after a disaster occurs.

   A. Determine the source of the disaster.

   B. Identify the resources that must be replaced immediately.

   C. Declare a disaster.

   D. Determine how long it will take to bring critical functions back online.

32. Which team is responsible for determining the scope and severity of the damage caused?

   A. Damage assessment team

   B. BCP team

   C. Salvage team

   D. Restoration team

33. Which team is responsible for beginning the recovery of the original site?

    A. Damage assessment team

    B. BCP team

    C. Salvage team

    D. Restoration team

34. Which of the following time is the recovery time objective?

    A. 48 hours

    B. 28 hours

    C. 20 hours

    D. 1 hour

35. In this scenario, what would the 60-minute time period be referred to as?

    A. Recovery point objective

    B. Recovery time period

    C. Maximum tolerable downtime

    D. Recovery point time period

36. Which characteristic denotes the evidence having a whole truth?

    A. Complete

    B. Reliable

    C. Relevant

    D. Sufficient

37. Which characteristic refers to the evidence consistent with facts?

    A. Complete

    B. Reliable

C. Relevant

D. Sufficient

38. What would the 60-minute time period be referred to as?

A. Recovery time period

B. Maximum tolerable downtime

C. Recovery point objective

D. Recovery point time period

39. Which of the following involves the proper collection of relevant data during the incident response process and includes analysis, interpretation, reaction, and recovery?

A. Chain of custody

B. Due care

C. Investigation

D. Motive, opportunity, and means

40. Which level is associated with striping and mirroring?

A. RAID level 0

B. RAID level 3

C. RAID level 5

D. RAID level 10

41. Which RAID level is a most commonly used mode that employs block-level striping and interleaving parity across all disks?

A. RAID level 0

B. RAID level 3

C. RAID level 5

D. RAID level 10

42. From some operations-security criteria, which of the following is one of the key areas when dealing with software?

A. Enabling of local administrator rights

B. Software licensing

C. Enabling automatic updates

D. Changing time zones

43. Which one of the following is not the protection control types?

A. Recovery

B. Response

C. Deterrent

D. Corrective

44. Which type of protection control is used to discourage violations?

A. Recovery

B. Response

C. Deterrent

D. Corrective

45. RAID level 5 indicates the following?

A. Hamming-code parity

B. Byte-level parity

C. Block-level parity

D. Interleave parity

46. What is the most common cause of loss of intellectual property?

    A. Negligence

    B. Espionage

    C. Pirating

    D. Virus

47. Which of the following is the suitable example of a technical deterrent?

    A. Disaster recovery plan

    B. Warning banner

    C. Supervision

    D. IDS

48. Which of the following is the suitable example of a technical detective?

    A. Disaster recovery plan

    B. Warning banner

    C. Supervision

    D. IDS

49. Which of the following is not one of those levels of assurance?

    A. Trusted recovery

    B. System integrity

    C. Trusted facility management

    D. Confidential operations

50. What term describes information that may remain on computer media after it has been deleted?

    A. Data remanence

B. Shadowing

C. Mirroring

D. Ghosting

Chapter 8: Software Development Security

1. Which system development model based on the Waterfall development methodology?
    A. Spiral
    B. Agile
    C. V-shaped
    D. Incremental

2. Which of the following is a valid system development methodology?
    A. The spring model
    B. The spiral model
    C. The production model
    D. The Gantt model

3. Which model has the goal to develop a systematic framework for creating quality software that lets measurable and repeatable results?
    A. Agile Model
    B. V-shaped Model
    C. Capability Maturity Model
    D. Rapid Application Development Model

4. Which of the following is the third level of the Capability Maturity Model Integration?
    A. Repeatable
    B. Optimizing
    C. Managed
    D. Defined

5. Which Capability Maturity Model (CMM) focuses on continuous process improvement?
    A. Level 4: Managed
    B. Level 5: Optimizing

    C. Level 2: Repeatable

    D. Level 3: Defined

6. Which one of the following is not an element of the DevOps model?
    A. Information security
    B. Software development
    C. Quality assurance
    D. IT operations

7. What component of the change management process allows developers to prioritize activities?
    A. Release control
    B. Configuration control
    C. Request control
    D. Change audit

8. GitHub, Bitbucket, and SourceForge are the example of
    A. Secure coding
    B. Code repositories
    C. Security controls
    D. Configuration management

9. Which one of the following does not measure the change management process?
    A. Request control
    B. Release control
    C. Configuration audit
    D. Change control

10. Which of the following best defines the term DevOps?
    A. The practice of incorporating development, IT, and quality assurance (QA) staff into software development projects.
    B. A multidisciplinary development team with representatives from many or all the stakeholder populations.
    C. The operationalization of software development activities to support just-in-time delivery.
    D. A software development methodology that relies more on the use of operational prototypes than on extensive upfront planning.

11. After processing through the SDLC phases, the next step of the released product follows:
    A. Configuration management
    B. Operation
    C. Maintenance
    D. Both B and C

12. When should security first be addressed in a project?
    A. During requirements development
    B. During integration testing
    C. During design specifications
    D. During implementation

13. In the development life cycle, what strategy should be used to avoid risk?
    A. Documentation
    B. Mitigation
    C. Addressed
    D. Ignored

14. Security controls must be measured at which phases of the software life cycle?
    A. Design analysis, software development, installation, and implementation
    B. Project initiation, software development, and operation maintenance
    C. Design specifications
    D. All of the above

15. _____ is a maturity model for evaluating and improving the software development process.
    A. Capability Maturity Model Integration
    B. System development life cycle
    C. ISO/IEC 27002
    D. Certification and accreditation processes

16. The process of recording changes made to systems is known as:
    A. Change Review Board
    B. System Maintenance

    C. Change Management

    D. Configuration Management

17. Which organization publishes a list of the Top 25 Most Dangerous Software Errors that can cause weaknesses and vulnerabilities in an application?

    A. OWASP

    B. CCB

    C. MITRE

    D. NIST

18. Which of the following software development models is an iterative model?

    A. Spiral

    B. Agile

    C. V-shaped

    D. Incremental

19. The following list provides various phases of system security life cycle except:

    1. Integration phase

    2. Initiation phase

    3. Implementation phase

    4. Disposal phase

20. Who publishes a short list of security standards that organizations should adopt?

    1. OWASP

    2. CCB

    3. MITRE

    4. NIST

21. Which vulnerability allows a third party execution of web scripting languages within the security context of a trusted site?

    A. Cross-site request forgery (CSRF)

    B. SQL injection

    C. PHP remote file inclusion (RFI)

    D. Cross-site scripting (XSS)

22. A database contains an item with an empty primary key. What database concept has been violated?

    A. Normalization

    B. Entity integrity

    C. Referential integrity

    D. Semantic integrity

23. A database contains every foreign key match the primary key. What database concept has been followed?

    A. Normalization

    B. Entity integrity

    C. Referential integrity

    D. Semantic integrity

24. What designates a more agile development and support model, where developers directly support operations?

    A. Spiral

    B. Sashimi

    C. DevOps

    D. Waterfall

25. Which type of approach taken by the software development company to develop new apps for mobile?

    A. ISO/IEC 27002

    B. System development life cycle

    C. Capability Maturity Model Integration

    D. Certification and accreditation processes

26. Who addresses and maintain the software development system throughout the development life cycle?

    A. ISO/IEC 27002

    B. System development life cycle

    C. Capability Maturity Model Integration

    D. Certification and accreditation processes

27. Who creates and maintain the organizational information security management system?

    A. ISO/IEC 27002

B. System development life cycle

C. Capability Maturity Model Integration

D. Certification and accreditation processes

28. Which of the following detection methods is an effective way to detect malicious software or activity pattern?

   A. Behavior blocking

   B. Signature-based detection

   C. Fingerprint detection

   D. Heuristic detection

29. Which of the following detection methods evaluates the overall structure of the executable code?

   A. Behavior blocking

   B. Signature-based detection

   C. Fingerprint detection

   D. Heuristic detection

30. The methodology of employing an integrated product team (IPT) for software development is designed to attain which of the following objectives?

   A. Developing and testing software with fewer security flaws

   B. Developing and testing software best suitable to the deployment environment

   C. Developing and testing software with fewer defective features

   D. Developing and testing software that will be most profitable

31. Of the following steps that define the development of a botnet, which best describes the step that comes first?

   A. The infected server sends attack commands to the botnet.

   B. Spammer pays a hacker for the use of a botnet.

   C. Controller server instructs infected systems to send spam to mail servers.

   D. Malicious code is sent out that has bot software as its payload.

32. What type of cross-site scripting vulnerability is the standard structure layout to represent HTML and XML documents?

   A. Second order

   B. DOM-based

C. Persistent

D. Nonpersistent

33. Which of the following is an invalid database management system model?

A. The structured database management system

B. The hierarchical database management system

C. The network database management system

D. The relational database management system

34. Which of the following is an invalid form of application control?

A. Preventive

B. Corrective

C. Detective

D. Constructive

35. Which of the following is the part of the Database Management System?

A. Views

B. Object-oriented interfaces

C. Tables

D. Schemas

36. Choose the correct order of software capability maturity model level from the following options?

A. Initiating, repeatable, defined, managed, optimizing

B. Initiating, defined, repeatable, managed, optimizing

C. Initiating, defined, repeatable, optimizing, managed

D. Initiating, repeatable, defined, optimizing, managed

37. What is the most common problem faced by audit logs?

A. Audit logs are collected but not analyzed.

B. Audit logs use parsing tools that distort the correct record of events.

C. Audit logs are not backed up.

D. Audit logs can be observed only by auditors.

38. Which type of database integrates related records and fields into a logical tree structure?

A. Relational

B. Object-oriented

C. Hierarchical

D. Network

39. Which term describes the storage of data from multiple sources?

A. Atomicity

B. Metadata

C. Data mining

D. Data warehousing

40. Which type of document has signed in software escrow?

A. A form of insurance

B. A form of a maintenance agreement

C. An offsite backup

D. A clustered software service

41. Which of the following is not helpful in assessing the security of acquired software?

A. The reliability and maturity of the vendor

B. Third-party vulnerability assessments

C. In-house code reviews

D. The NIST's National Software Reference Library

42. _____ is a software testing technique that delivers invalid, unexpected, or random data to the input interfaces of a program.

A. Fuzz testing

B. Structured testing

C. Agile testing

D. EICAR

43. Which of the following represents rows and columns within relational databases?

A. Rows and tuples

B. Attributes and rows

C. Tuples and attributes

D. Keys and views

44. What type of database software integrity service promises that tuples are uniquely recognized by primary key values?
    A. Entity integrity
    B. Referential integrity
    C. Concurrent integrity
    D. Semantic integrity

45. Which of the following antimalware detection methods monitors suspicious code as it executes within the operating system?
    A. Behavior blocking
    B. Fingerprint detection
    C. Signature-based detection
    D. Heuristic detection

46. Which of the following is another name for Persistent XSS vulnerability?
    A. Second-order vulnerability
    B. DOM-based vulnerability
    C. Cross-site scripting (XSS)
    D. None of the above

47. What type of testing involves to validate data structure, logic, and boundary conditions?
    A. Acceptance testing
    B. Regression testing
    C. Integration testing
    D. Unit testing

48. Which type of application testing ensures the coding that meets customer requirements?
    A. Acceptance testing
    B. Regression testing
    C. Integration testing
    D. Unit testing

49. At which level of the CMM are processed expected to be inconsistent and depend heavily on institutional knowledge?

A. Level 1
B. Level 2
C. Level 3
D. Level 4

50. Which of the following is considered as a middleware technology?
   A. Atomicity
   B. CORBA
   C. OLE
   D. Object-oriented programming

Answers

Chapter 1

1. A. Unauthorized disclosure

   Explanation: Confidentiality is one of the most important components of the CIA triad and Information Assurance (IA) pillars. Confidentiality is all about preventing the disclosure of sensitive information to unauthorized peoples. The only authorized user can access the resources and protected data.

2. A. Acquisition

   Explanation: The acquisition process is when two organizations decide to merge into a single organization or when an organization purchases another one.

3. B. Divestiture

   Explanation: The divestiture is a process when a part of an organization is sold or separated. It is a challenge for a security professional to ensure the security.

4. A. CSO

   Explanation: CSO is responsible for monitoring, motivation and directing the security committees.

5. D. Information Asset Owners (IAOs)

   Explanation: Information Asset Owners (IAOs) are those individuals, usually managers, who are responsible for the protection of information assets. They are accountable for this security by the Security Committee (SC) or local Security Committee (LSC).

6. B. Pharming

Explanation: Pharming is a type of cyber-attack in which a user is redirected to a malicious website created by the attacker. Generally, this type of redirection happens without user acceptance or knowledge.

7. A. Phishing

Explanation: Phishing is a type of cybercrime in which a user is lured to an attacker created an illegitimate website that looks similar to the actual website the user intended to visit.

8. A. Data Across National Borders

Explanation: The transfer of computerized data across national borders, states or political boundaries are termed as the transborder data flow. The data may be personal, business, technical, and organizational.

9. B. Trademark

Explanation: A unique symbol or mark that is used to represent an individual's or organization's product is known as Trademark.

10. A. Business Impact Analysis (BIA)

Explanation: A Business Impact Analysis (BIA) works as functional analysis, in which a team collects data through interviews and documentary sources; documents business functions, activities, and transactions; develop a hierarchy of business functions, and finally apply a classification scheme to indicate each function's criticality level.

11. B. Detective Control

Explanation: Detective Control is the control designed for troubleshooting or identifying the error, issues, and irregularities. These controls are effective after the incident.

12. A. Security Control Assessment (SCA)

Explanation: Security Control Assessment are the principals which ensure the security policies enforced in an organization are meeting their goals and objectives. Security Control Assessment evaluates these security policies implementers and responsible for information system if they are complying with stated security goals. SCA evaluates management, operational, and

technical security controls in an information system to identify correct and effective enforcement of these controls.

13. B. Non-Physical Assets

Explanation: Intangible assets are non-physical assets. This category includes assets such as software, source codes, intellectual property of an organization & it is trade secrets. This category also includes personal identification information such as personal information of customers.

14. A. SD Elements

Explanation: SD Element is a threat modeling tool by Security Compas.

15. E. None of the above

16. A. STRIDE

Explanation: STRIDE is a methodology of threat modeling developed by Microsoft focusing on computer security threats.

17. C. Risk management committee

18. B. Top secret

Explanation: Top-secret is the highest level of business and military data classification.

19. C. Authenticated user

Explanation: Files, database tables, and tax forms are examples of objects, an authenticated user is the example of subjects.

20. B. Advance and protect the profession

Explanation: The canons are applied in order, and final, therefore least important canon wants professionals to advance and protect the profession.

21. D. COBIT is a model for IT governance.

Explanation: COBIT is to provide management and business process owners with Information Technology (IT) governance model that supports in delivering value from IT and understanding and managing the risks related to IT.

22. ITIL is an infrastructure for providing best services in IT.

Explanation: ITIL® (Information Technology Infrastructure Library) is a framework for providing best services in IT Service Management (ITSM).

23. C. Service Transition

Explanation: Service Transition describes taking new projects and making them operational.

24. B. The level of insurance required to cover the asset

Explanation: The level of insurance required to cover the asset is not determine when assigning values to assets.

25. A. Mean time to repair

Explanation: Mean time to Repair (MTTR) is the amount of time it will be expected to take to get a system fixed and back into production.

26. C. Project initiation phase

Explanation: Project initiation phase is how the actual planning of the business continuity plan begins.

27. B. Business impact analysis

Explanation: Business Impact Analysis (BIA) is conducted after the BCP team has achieved management's support for their efforts.

28. D. Identify vulnerabilities and threats to business functions

Explanation: Identifying vulnerabilities and threats to business functions takes place at the end of a Business Impact Analysis.

29. A. parallel or full-interruption test

Explanation: Parallel and full-interruption tests are not part of a BIA. These tests are related to Business Continuity Planning.

30. B. Develop the continuity planning policy statement.

Explanation: Developing the continuity planning policy statement includes writing a policy that provides the guidance needed to develop a business continuity plan and that assigns authority to the necessary roles to continue

these tasks.

31. C. The extraction of data to share with unauthorized entities.

   Explanation: The extraction of data to share with unauthorized entities is a confidentiality issue, not an integrity issue.

32. D. The extraction of data to share with unauthorized entities.

   Explanation: The extraction of data to share with unauthorized entities is a confidentiality issue.

33. B. Discontinuing activities that generate risk

   Explanation: Discontinuing activities that generate risk is a way of responding to risk through avoidance.

34. D. Security regulating committee

   Explanation: Person is joining a security regulating committee, which is accountable for making decisions on tactical and strategic security issues within the enterprise.

35. Risk transference. Share the risk with other entities.

   Explanation: Risk can be dealt with in four basic ways: transfer it, avoid it,

36. C. Reconstitution phase

   Explanation: When it is time for the company to move back into its original site or a new site, the company is ready to go into the reconstitution phase.

37. A. Risk mitigation

   Explanation: By Risk mitigation process, the company has reduced the risk when

   implementing security controls.

38. A. Public

   Explanation: The business data classification scheme has

   four levels, of which the lowest is public. The other three answers are part of the government's data classification scheme.

39. A. Auditor

Explanation: Auditors are responsible for reviewing and examine policies and procedures.

40. C. Infosec security officer

    Explanation: The infosec security officer has delegated the responsibility of implementing and maintaining security by the organization's senior-level management.

41. C. Controlled

    Explanation: Controlled is not including in military level.

42. Answer: A & B. Proprietary & Classified

    Explanation: Classified and proprietary are not part of either data classification.

43. B. Abstraction

    Explanation: Abstraction is used to remove complexity.

44. D. Data hiding

    Explanation: Data hiding is the process of revealing only external properties to other components.

45. C. Displacement

    Explanation: Risk cannot be displaced.

46. A. Risk analysis

    Explanation: Risk analysis is the method of identifying vulnerabilities and threats and assessing the possible damage to determine where to implement security precautions.

47. B. Threat * Vulnerability * Asset Value (AV) = Total Risk

    Explanation: The formula for total risk is Threat * Vulnerability * Asset Value (AV) = Total Risk.

48. C. Procedures

    Explanation: Procedures are detailed in that they give the operator explicit instructions on how to perform specific operations, providing a step-by-step

guide.

49. D. Redundant array of inexpensive disks (RAID)

   Explanation: Redundant Array of Inexpensive Disks (RAID) helps protect availability.

50. D. Commercial

   Explanation: The commercial form of data classification uses four levels to classify data: "confidential," "private," "sensitive," and "public."

Chapter 2

1. C. Authority

Explanation: The main purpose of data classification is to specify the level of confidentiality, integrity, and availability protection required for each type of dataset.

2. B. Officer

Explanation: Asset classification is based on the Owners, Custodian, and Users, not by the Officer.

3. C. Custodian

Explanation: Custodian provides practical protection of assets such as data.

4. C. licensee

Explanation: The entity that processes, stores, or transmits the information on behalf of the owner is called a licensee.

5. C. Residual Data

Explanation: Data that remains even after erasing or formatting digital media is called Residual Data

6. D. System owner

Explanation: The System Owner is a manager responsible for the particular computer that holds data. It includes the hardware and software configuration, updates, patching, and others.

7. C. Maintenance

Explanation: Maintenance is a regular process to ensure that the data in the storage media is not corrupted or damaged.

8. C. Data Destruction

Explanation: Data destruction is done by way of formatting the media.

9. C. Storage control

Explanation: Storage control belongs to protecting data in media.

10. B. BIOS checks

Explanation: BIOS checks help in password protection during the boot up process.

11. B. Data with personnel

Explanation: The above statement related to Data with personnel that focuses on the individual should be secured.

12. B. Data at rest

Explanation: Hard disk drives (HDDs), solid-state drives (SSDs), optical discs (CD/DVD), or magnetic tape related with Data at rest.

13. A. Data in motion

Explanation: Data in motion is data that is moving between computing nodes over a data network such as the Internet.

14. C. Data at rest

Explanation: In data at rest state; protection strategies include secure access controls, the segregation of duties, and the implementation of the need to know mechanisms for sensitive data.

15. D. ISO 27002

Explanation: ISO 17799 was renumbered to ISO 27002 in 2005, to make it consistent with the 27000 series of ISO security standards.

16. B. COBIT

Explanation: There are 34 Information Technology processes across the four domains in COBIT.

17. C. Phase 3

Explanation: Phase 3 conducts the Risk Analysis and develops the risk mitigation strategy.

18. C. Scoping

Explanation: Scoping is the process of determining which an organization will employ portions of a standard.

19. C. Hashing

Explanation: Hashing method of data protection will ensure integrity.

20. D. Ensure data has proper security labels

Explanation: Data owners determine data sensitivity labels.

21. C. Verifying the availability of data

Explanation: The responsibility of verifying the availability of data is the only responsibility mentioned that does not belong to the data owner.

22. A. Extracting data from a database

Explanation: Data classification does not involve the extraction of data from a database.

23. B. Ensuring the protection of customer, company, and employee data

Explanation: The CPO is responsible for ensuring the security of customer, company, and employee data, which keeps the company free from legal trial.

24. D. Data user

Explanation: Any individual who uses data for work-related tasks is a data user. Users must have the basic level of accessibility to the data to perform the responsibilities.

25. How will the data be used?

Explanation: How the data will be used has no bearing on how sensitive it is.

26. A. Understand the different levels of protection that must be provided

Explanation: While developing a company's data classification program, first understand the different levels of protection that must be provided.

27. A. Cost/benefit analysis

Explanation: An analysis of each possible measure's cost and benefit can determine which course of action should be taken.

28. B. Determine the data classification

Explanation: Determine the data classification is the chief security responsibility.

29. A. Data specification and classification

Explanation: Determination of what the data is, and its classification, is the first essential phase of being able to provide it with the appropriate level of protection.

30. B. Degaussing

Explanation: The physical destruction of the device is the only effective way to ensure no data remains on an SSD.

31. C. Top secret, Secret, Confidential, Unclassified

Explanation: Within the U.S. military complex and national security apparatus, the most common placement for data classification are unclassified vs. classified. Within the classifications for classified information are Confidential, Secret, and Top Secret.

32. C. Purging via overwriting

Explanation: Purging means making data unavailable even by physical forensic efforts.

33. A. Hospitals

Explanation: Having a hospital nearby can be considered an asset. This allows the company to get help to anyone who is injured quickly.

34. C. Carbon dioxide sensing

Explanation: CO_2 sensing is not a valid type of fire detection.

35. A. UPS

Explanation: An uninterruptible power supply (UPS) can be used to provide power to critical equipment during a short power failure.

36. C. Brownouts

Explanation: A power degradation, such as a brownout, occurs when power companies experience an increasingly high demand for power.

37. B. Layered access control

Explanation: Access control is the key to physical security, and it works best when deployed in layers.

38. A. Legal liability

Explanation: Guard dogs cannot differentiate between authorized and unauthorized personnel, so they can be a legal liability that results in criminal charges.

39. C. Proximity badges

Explanation: Proximity identification can be used to activate doors to identify employees. These systems only require users to pass in proximity to the sensing system.

40. A. Social engineering

Explanation: Social engineering is a type of attack in which intruders attempt to gain physical access to the valuable facility by exploiting people's generally trusting nature.

41. D Server rooms should be accessible to all IT staff.

Explanation: Server rooms are usually inaccessible to all IT staff because their actions should be done remotely. Access should be allowed for only the minimum number of staff authorized to access the server room.

42. C. Defense in layers

Explanation: A contingency plan protects you when a primary control fails; it represents the concept of multiple layers in your defense.

43. B Cipher lock

Explanation: cipher lock is considered the most secure type of lock.

44. A. Formatting

Explanation: Formatting is the least effective way to sanitize media such as hard drives.

45. C. Blackouts

Explanation: A power outage, which can be called a blackout, is when power is lost for an extended time.

46. D. All the above

Explanation: Cryptography can be effective control of every phase in the information life cycle.

47. D. Maintenance

Explanation: Maintenance requirements does not relate data retention policy address.

48. C. Senior management

Explanation: Senior management always carries the ultimate responsibility for the organization.

49. C. Confidentiality, Integrity, and Availability

Explanation: While classifying the data, the data owner must evaluate the availability, integrity, and confidentiality requirements.

50. Acceptable use policies

Explanation: Data retention policies should be the primary reason for the disposal of most of our information.

Chapter 3

1. A. Storage Root Key (SRK)

Explanation: Each TPM has a master wrapping key which is known as Storage Root Key (SRK), stored in TPM itself.

2. B. Endorsement Key (EK)

Explanation: Endorsement Key (EK), A public/private key pair that is installed in the TPM at the time of manufacture and cannot be modified.

3. A.2

Explanation: TPM's internal memory is divided into two different segments:

    1. Persistent (static) memory modules.
    2. Versatile (dynamic) memory modules.

4. Protects memory from being access by unauthorized programs.

Explanation: Memory Protection domain associated with the protection of memory from unauthorized access and modification of the content stored in it by different programs or processes.

5. C. Subject

Explanation: The subject is any user or process which generates the request to access a resource.

6. C. Proxy server

Explanation: A user connects with the web proxy server to access these restricted sites.

7. A. IDEA

Explanation: Asymmetric key algorithms include RSA, Diffie-Hellman, El Gamal, DSA, and Elliptic Curve.

8. A. 2

Explanation: There are two different types of access controls which can be implemented, Mandatory Access Control (MAC) and Discretionary Access Control (DAC).

9. B. Assurance focus on security management

Explanation: ISO/IEC 27001 assurance focus on security management

10. B. Trusted System

Explanation: A trusted system covers all layers of protection and its integrated security mechanisms, control and concepts are reliable.

11. B. Bell-LaPadula

Explanation: The Bell-LaPadula model works with a multilevel security system.

12. D. 8

Explanation: There are eight rules in Graham-Denning Model.

13. B. Brewer and Nash Model

Explanation: The Brewer and Nash models are also known as the Chinese Wall model.

14. A. Biba

Explanation: The Biba model is a security model that addresses the integrity of data within a system.

15. B. TCSEC

Explanation: TCSEC is the formal implementation of the Bell-LaPadula model.

16. C. EAL

Explanation: The Common Criteria uses a different assurance rating system than the previously used criteria. These ratings and packages are called Evaluation Assurance Levels (EALs).

17. D. TCG

Explanation: TPM chip was devised by the Trusted Computing Group (TCG).

18. A. Mandatory access control

Explanation: Sensitivity labels are a fundamental component in the Mandatory access control type of access control systems.

19. C. Cryptanalysis

Explanation: The process of finding vulnerabilities in code, an encryption algorithm, or key management scheme is called Cryptanalysis.

20. B. Rubber Hose Attack

Explanation: Rubber hose attack is a technique of gaining information about cryptographic secret such as passwords, keys, encrypted files, by torturing a person.

21. A. PLCs

Explanation: Programmable logic controllers (PLCs) connect to the sensors and convert sensor data to digital data exclude telemetry hardware.

22. A. IaaS

Explanation: IaaS model offers cloud-based infrastructure to deploy remote data center.

23. C. Community

Explanation: Community Clouds are accessed by multiple parties having common goals and shared resources.

24. B. Data Encryption Standard

Explanation: Data Encryption Standard was developed by NIST and the NSA to encrypt sensitive but unclassified government data.

25. A. HMAC

Explanation: When an HMAC function is used, a symmetric key is united with the message, and then that result is put through a hashing algorithm.

26. A. 16

Explanation: DES algorithm is consisting of 16 rounds processing the data with the 16 intermediary round keys of 48-bit generated from 56-bit cipher key by a Round Key Generator.

27. D. A method to let the receiver of the message prove the source and integrity of a message

Explanation: A digital signature is a simple way to verify the authenticity and integrity of a message.

28. B. RSA

Explanation: RSA algorithm uses a product of two large prime numbers to derive the key pairs.

29. B. 1024

Explanation: A 160-bit EC key is equivalent to a 1,024-bit RSA key.

30. A and B., The sender, generates the hash of plaintext with a public key
& The sender encrypts the hash with a private key

Explanation: The sender generates a hash of the plaintext and encrypts the hash with a private key.

31. C. Integrity

Explanation: While EMI issues like crosstalk could impact all aspects listed, it most commonly impacts integrity.

32. D. Graham-Denning

Explanation: The Graham-Denning model addresses how access rights between subjects and objects are defined, developed, and integrated.

33. A. Data Execution Prevention

Explanation: Data Execution Prevention (DEP) is a security feature included in modern operating systems. It is intended to prevent a process from executing code from a non-executable memory region.

34. C. The CA signs the certificate.

Explanation: A Certificate Authority (CA) is a trusted organization that maintains and issues digital certificates.

35. B. Public key cryptography is another name for asymmetric cryptography, while public key infrastructure consists of public key cryptographic mechanisms.

Explanation: Public key cryptography is asymmetric cryptography; the terms are used interchangeably. While public key cryptography is one piece in public key infrastructure (PKI).

36. C. Keys are generated from a master key.

Explanation: For complex keys generation, commonly a master key is created and then symmetric keys are generated from it.

37. D. It is more efficient.

Explanation: An elliptic curve cryptosystem (ECC) differs from other asymmetric algorithms due to its efficiency.

38. A. One-time pad

Explanation: One-time pad works similarly to stream cipher, both working on to provide protection

39. B. Digital signature

Explanation: A message can be digitally signed, which provides authentication, non-repudiation, and integrity.

40. B. Bulk data encryption

Explanation: The Advanced Encryption Standard (AES) is a data encryption standard that was developed to improve upon the previous standard—the Data Encryption Standard (DES).

41. B. 520

Explanation: The formula for determining the number of keys required in this environment is N × 2, which is the number of people (N) multiplied by the number of keys each person would need (2). So, 260*2=520

42. A. Confidentiality

Explanation: The Take-Grant system model addresses confidentiality. It uses rights for this process that are divided into four basic operations: create, revoke, grant, and take.

43. D. Verified design

Explanation: The name for TCSEC A1 specification has verified the design.

44. A. Trusted path requirements

Explanation: B2 systems possess Trusted path requirements.

45. C. Seven assurance levels

Explanation: Common Criteria (CC) defines seven assurance levels. CC was designed as a way to improve assurance efforts between Europe and North America.

46. D. EAL 7

Explanation: EAL 7 is formally verified, designed, and tested.

47. B. Information Technology Security Evaluation Criteria (ITSEC)

Explanation: ITSEC was developed in the late 1980s to address the needs of the European Union.

48. C. Brewer and Nash

Explanation: Brewer and Nash address conflicts of interest.

49. A. Key exchange

Explanation: After a session key has been created, the key must be exchanged securely.

50. B. The message digest has been altered.

Explanation: Hashing algorithms generate message digests to detect whether an alteration has taken place.

Chapter 4

1. C. Physical, Data Link, Network, Transport, Session, Presentation, Application

Explanation: The OSI model layers from bottom to top are: Physical, Data Link, Network, Transport, Session, Presentation, and Application.

2. B. Data Link Layer

Explanation: The function performed on the data within the Data Link layer includes adding the source and destination MAC addresses to the frame.

3. D. 24-bits

Explanation: The Media Access Control (MAC) address has a 48-bit (6-byte) hexadecimal representation, 24 bits represent the vendor or manufacturer of the physical network interface, also known as Organizationally Unique Identifier (OUI).

4. A. Simple Key Management for Internet Protocols (SKIP)

Explanation: SKIP functioning at layer 3.

5. C. Gateway

Explanation: A network device that works at the Application layer, namely, the gateway.

6. B. Link

Explanation: Link layer corresponds to the Physical and Data-Link Layer of the OSI model.

7. C. 65,534

Explanation: a full class B subnet supports 65,534 hosts.

8. B. Covert channels are allowed.

Explanation: Covert channels are allowed, describe as a drawback of Multilayer Protocol.

9. A. MPLS

Explanation: MPLS is designed to handle a wide range of protocols through encapsulation.

10. D. RTP

Explanation: Common VoIP protocols include Real-time Transport Protocol (RTP), designed to carry streaming audio and video.

11. B. AES

Explanation: SRTP uses AES for confidentiality.

12. B. Confidentiality

Explanation: WEP uses an RC4 stream cipher for confidentiality.

13. B. OSA

Explanation: WPA uses the Temporal Key Integrity Protocol (TKIP) to address some of the encryption problems in WEP.

14. A. Shared Key Authentication

Explanation: Shared Key Authentication (SKA) uses a four-way handshake to authenticate.

15. C. TFTP, ARP, IP, and UDP

Explanation: The listed protocols work at these associated layers: TFTP (application), ARP (data link), IP (network), and UDP (transport).

16. D. Remote Desktop Console Access

Explanation: Two common modern protocols providing for remote access to a desktop are Virtual Network Computing (VNC), which typically runs on TCP 5900, and Remote Desktop Protocol (RDP), which typically runs on TCP port 3389.

17. B. Content Distribution Network

Explanation: Content Distribution Networks (CDN) also called Content Delivery Networks. CDN uses a series of distributed caching servers to improve performance and lower the latency of downloaded online content.

18. B. Packet filtering

Explanation: A packet filter is a simple and fast firewall. It has no concept of "state": each filtering decision is made by a single packet.

19. A. Single mode

Explanation: Single-mode fiber is typically used for long-distance communication, over several kilometers or miles.

20. A. EAP-TLS

Explanation: EAP-TLS is the most secure (and costly) form of EAP because it requires both server and client-side certificates.

Chapter 4

21. D. NAT

Explanation: Accessing an IPv6 network through an IPv4 network is called tunneling.

22. A. Application-layer proxy firewall

Explanation: Application-layer firewalls are the most secure, as they can filter based on OSI Layers 3–7.

23. B. MAC address

Explanation: Restricting Bluetooth device discovery relies on the 48-bit Bluetooth MAC address.

24. D LLC and MAC

Explanation: Logic Layer Control (LLC) and Media Access Control (MAC) are the two sublayers of Layer 2

25. B IEEE 802.2 and 802.3

Explanation: Two standard specifications of layer 2 are IEEE 802.2 and 802.3

26. A. PPTP

Explanation: PPTP provides the best solution for VPN tunneling.

27. B. It is usually used to send unsolicited messages.

Explanation: Bluetooth is vulnerable to an attack called Bluejacking, which entails an attacker sending an unsolicited message to a device that is Bluetooth-enabled.

28. C. IGRP

Explanation: Interior Gateway Routing Protocol (IGRP) is a distance-vector routing protocol that was developed by, and is proprietary to, Cisco Systems.

29. B. Softphones are more secure than IP phones.

Explanation: Softphones are not securable as compared to IP telephones

30. A. Security

Explanation: VoIP does not provide secure communication, while it is cost effective and flexible way of communication.

31. B. Temporal Key Integrity Protocol

Explanation: TKIP works with the Wired Equivalent Privacy (WEP) protocol by feeding it keying material, which is data to be used for generating new dynamic keys.

32. C. DNSSEC

Explanation: DNSSEC is a set of extensions to DNS that provides to DNS clients origin authentication of DNS data to reduce the threat of DNS poisoning, spoofing, and similar attack types.

33. D. Content distribution network (CDN)

Explanation: Content Distribution Networks (CDNs) are aimed to optimize the delivery of content, primarily via the Hypertext Transfer Protocol (HTTP), to clients based on their global topological position.

34. C. Session Initiation Protocol (SIP)

Explanation: The Session Initiation Protocol is commonly used for all VoIP transactions except the actual media exchange between calling or receiving stations.

35. B. Data link layer

Explanation: The Point-to-Point Tunneling Protocol (PPTP) is a way of applying Virtual Private Networks (VPNs). It is a Microsoft-proprietary VPN protocol that works at the data link layer of the OSI model.

36. C. Distributed Network Protocol 3 (DNP3)

Explanation: DNP3 was the protocol designed to perform multiple tasks at once.

37. D. TLS is the open-community version of SSL.

Explanation: SSL is a proprietary protocol, and TLS was developed by a standards body, making it an open-community protocol.

38. B. IP spoofing is used to hijack SSL and IPSec secure communications.

Explanation: Secure Sockets Layer (SSL) and IPSec can protect the integrity, authenticity, and confidentiality of network traffic.

39. D. Blacklists are undependable.

Explanation: E-mail spoofing is easy to execute because SMTP lacks an adequate authentication mechanism.

40. B. 2.4 GHz and 54 Mbps

Explanation: 802.11g is 2.4 GHz and 54 Mbps.

41. D. Unicast

Explanation: All data transmissions must generate from a single source. As such, only a unicast can be both a source and a destination address.

42. A. Anycast

Explanation: Anycast is a technology associated with IPv6.

43. A. Router

Explanation: Routers are the primary equipment of this layer and are responsible for routing IP.

44. A. Plain-text passwords

Explanation: Plaintext usernames and passwords are a major security issue with email.

45. C. PAP

Explanation: Password Authentication Protocol (PAP) is the least secure type of authentication listed. It is insecure because it sends credentials in plaintext.

46. D. EAP-TTLS

Explanation: EAP-Tunnelled Transport Layer Security (EAP-TTLS) is an EAP protocol that extends TLS.

47. A. IEEE 802.16

Explanation: IEEE 802.16 is a WiMAX wireless standard that allows wireless traffic to cover a wide geographical area.

48. A. Circuit

Explanation: Circuit-based proxy firewalls make decisions based on header information, not the protocol's command structure.

49. B. DHCP snooping

Explanation: DHCP snooping ensures that DHCP servers can assign IP addresses to only selected systems, identified by their MAC addresses.

50. C. SIP

Explanation: The Session Initiation Protocol (SIP) is an IETF-designed signaling protocol, extensively used for controlling multimedia communication sessions such as voice and video calls over IP.

Chapter 5

1.   E. None of the above

Explanation: All of the answers are included in the types of assets that an organization would try to protect with access controls.

2.   B. Centralized Access Control

Explanation: Centralized access control implies that a single entity within a system performs all authorization verification.

3.   B. Biometrics

Explanation: Physical biometric methods such as fingerprints, palm scan, and iris scans provide authentication for subjects.

4.   A. Something you have

Explanation: Something you have such as a Mobile phone is a type 2 authentication factor.

5.   C. Accountability

Explanation: Accountability is the ability to track users' actions as they access systems and data.

6. C. Metadata

Explanation: Metadata in an LDAP directory can be used for dynamic authentication systems.

7. A. Kerberos

Explanation: For authentication purpose, it uses Kerberos by default.

8. D. Session managing

Explanation: When using any type of authentication system, it's important to manage sessions to prevent unauthorized access.

9. A. Federated Identity management

Explanation: Federated identity management systems often use the Security Assertion Markup Language (SAML) and Service Provisioning Markup Language (SPML) to meet the challenges of common language.

10. C. Encrypting

Explanation: The management system secures the credentials with encryption to prevent unauthorized access.

11. C. Access control

Explanation: An access control model is a framework that directives how subjects access objects.

12. B. Nondiscretionary

Explanation: RBAC is a type of nondiscretionary access control because users do not have discretion regarding the groups of objects they are certified to access and are unable to transfer objects to other subjects.

13. A. Rule-based

Explanation: Rules of Rule-BAC are based on if/then statement.

14. D. MAC

Explanation: MAC is system-enforced access control based on a subject's clearance and an object's labels.

15. B. DAC

Explanation: Discretionary Access Control (DAC) model is implemented using Access Control Lists (ACLs) on objects.

16. C. ABAC

Explanation: Attribute Based Access Control (ABAC) is an advanced implementation of a Rule-BAC model.

17. D. Owner

Explanation: Discretionary Access Controls (DACs) system allows the owner, creator, or data custodian of an object to control and define access to the specified object.

18. B. Authentication

Explanation: Biometrics is a technology that validates an individual's identity by reading a physical attribute.

19. B. De-provisioning

Explanation: Deprovisioning is the act of removal or disables the user account. Deprovisioning performs rapid removal of access upon termination from the organization.

20. D. Discretionary

Explanation: The DAC model allows users, or data owners, the discretion of allowing other users to access their resources. DAC is applied by ACLs, which the data owner can configure.

21. D IDaaS

Explanation: Identity as a service (IDaaS) allows organizations to leverage cloud service for identity management.

22. A. Content-dependent access control

Explanation: Content-dependent access control uses the content, such as file contents, as an additional factor.

23. C. Context-dependent access control

Explanation: Context-dependent access control adds additional factors beyond username and password, such as the time of attempted access.

24. A. Kerberos

Explanation: Kerberos is a third-party authentication service that may be used to support single sign-on.

25. B. OpenID

Explanation: OpenID is a framework for exchanging authentication data, but it is not XML-based.

26. C. LDAP

Explanation: Lightweight directory access protocol is an open protocol for interfacing and querying directory service information from network operating systems using port 389 TCP or UDP.

27. A. XML

Explanation: is incorrect because XML (Extensible Markup Language) is a method for electronically coding documents and representing data structures such as those in web services. XML is not used to share security information.

28. D. GML

Explanation: Generalized Markup Language (GML) is a method created by IBM for formatting documents.

29. C. XACML

Explanation: Extensible Access Control Markup Language (XACML), which allows two or more organizations to share application security policies based upon their trust model.

30. B. An object

Explanation: An object is bound to an Access Control List (ACL), not a capability component.

31. A. A subject

Explanation: A capability table specifies the access rights a certain subject possesses about specific objects.

32. A. Detective control

Explanation: Investigations are a good example of a detective control.

33. B. Kerberos

Explanation: The best example of a capability table is Kerberos.

34. D. RBAC

Explanation: ore RBAC makes use of a many-to-many relationship and is useful in organizations that have well-defined roles.

35. D. Provisioning

Explanation: Provisioning is the management of user access.

36. A. Pretexting

Explanation: Pretexting is the act of using the established personal information to gain access to accounts, cell phone records, or other information.

37. D. Phishing

Explanation: Phishing is a nontechnical attack that attempts to trick the victim into giving up account or password information.

38. B. Kerberos

Explanation: Kerberos uses a key distribution center.

39. D. SESAME

Explanation: SESAME uses a Privilege Attribute Certificate (PAC) and TACACS, RADIUS not use PAC.

40. C. Kerberos

Explanation: The ticket-granting service is a component of Kerberos.

41. C. Biometrics

Explanation: Biometric systems are the most expensive means of performing authentication.

42. C. Mandatory access control

Explanation: Labels are associated with Mandatory Access Control (MAC).

43. B. Rule-based and mandatory

Explanation: Rule-based access control is most commonly seen in ACLs and is used with routers.

44. D. Corrective

Explanation: Corrective controls remove inappropriate actions.

45. C. Preventive

Explanation: A mantrap is a preventive control because it prevents the entry of unauthorized individuals.

46. B. Sniffing

Explanation: Sniffing is an example of a passive attack. Attackers perform sniff by simply wait and capture data.

47. A. Fingerprint recognition

Explanation: Fingerprints recognition are most closely associated with law enforcement.

48. C. Brute-force

> **Explanation**: Brute-force attacks are considered the most time-intensive type of offline password attack.
>
> 49. A. Something you remember
>
> **Explanation**: Something you remember is not included in the three primary types of authentication.
>
> 50. A. Authentication server
>
> **Explanation**: In a single sign-on method, all users are authenticating to one source. If that source goes down, authentication requests cannot be handled.

Chapter 6

1. C. Convene a management review

Explanation: The management review is not a part of any audit. Instead, this review typically uses the results of one or more audits to make strategic decisions.

2. A. Internal

Explanation: Internal assessment strategy should be aligned with the organization's business and day-to-day operations.

3. A. Internal

Explanation: An external audit strategy should complement the internal strategy, providing regular checks to ensure that procedures are being followed and the organization is meeting its compliance goals.

4. C. Personnel testing

Explanation: Social engineering is focused on people, so personnel testing is the best answer.

5. D. Vulnerability testing

Explanation: The goal of a vulnerability assessment is to identify elements in an environment that are not effectively protected.

6. A. Audit

Explanation: In the audit process, organizations compliance with PCI-DSS to meet their goals.

7. B. Mitigate risk

Explanation: The goal of a penetration test is to uncover weaknesses in security so they can be addressed to mitigate risk.

8. D. Vulnerability scanning

Explanation: Penetration testing goes through the vulnerability mapping instead of scanning.

9. A. Write Once Read Many (WORM)

Explanation: A log is a Write Once Read Many (WORM) type of data.

10. C. Synthetic transaction

Explanation: Synthetic transactions can be automated to run on a periodic basis to ensure the application is still performing as expected.

11. A. Code review

Explanation: Code review is the foundation of software assessment programs.

12. D. Misuse case testing

Explanation: Software and systems both can be tested for use other than its intended purpose; it is known as Misuse case testing.

13. B. Black box testing

Explanation: Black box testing has no prior knowledge of the environment being tested.

14. A. White box

Explanation: To fully test code, a white box test is required.

15. C. Creating accounts

Explanation: Account management does not only responsible for creating the user account but it also responsible for modifying with increasing vulnerabilities.

16. B. Backup verification

Explanation: The backup verification process ensures that backups are running properly and thus meeting the organization's data protection needs.

17. C. SOC 1 Type 2

Explanation: SOC 1 Type 2 reports are focused on the service organization's systems including a report about the suitability of the control operating effectively to meet its objective.

18. C. Third-party

Explanation: Third-party testing is specifically geared to ensuring that the internal and external auditors are properly following your policies and procedures.

19. C. SOC 3

Explanation: These reports are intended for users or clients requiring the assurance of control security, integrity & confidentiality of processes and availability. SOC3 reports can be distributed or published freely.

20. A. Security training is focused on skills, while security awareness training is focused on recognizing and responding to issues.

Explanation: Security training is the process of teaching a skill or set of skills that will allow people to better perform specific functions. While security awareness training is the process of exposing people to security issues so that they may be able to recognize them and better respond to them.

21. A. Integration testing

Explanation: Integration testing examines multiple software components as they are combined into a working system.

22. C. Acceptance testing

Explanation: Acceptance testing is designed to ensure the software meets the customer's operational requirements.

23. B. Fuzzing

Explanation: Fuzzing is a black-box testing method that does not require access to source code.

24. D. Normal operations are shut down.

Explanation: During full-interruption testing, normal operations are shut down.

25. C. Agents from each department come together and go through the test collectively.

Explanation: During a structured walk-through test, functional agents meet and review the plan to ensure its accuracy and that it properly and accurately reflects the company's recovery strategy by walking through it step-by-step.

26. D. Provisioning accounts, modifying accounts, auditing the use of accounts, and suspending accounts

Explanation: Provisioning accounts, modifying accounts, auditing the use of accounts, and suspending accounts are the key stages of account management.

27. C. Verifying account passwords, validating account usage, and deleting accounts

Explanation: Verifying account passwords, validating account usage, and deleting accounts are the stages of authentication management.

28. B. Making sure coders' work has been reviewed by other coders after they are done

Explanation: Code review is the process of reviewing code by other coders'.

29. A. To prevent against log tampering

Explanation: Event logs are usually one of the first things that an intruder will seek to modify to cover their tracks.

30. C. An executive summary that is comprehensive but does not exceed two pages

Explanation: The executive summary should never exceed two pages.

31. B. They enable management to understand the performance of a security program.

Explanation: The greatest value of security metrics is to establish the key performance indicators (KPIs) and key risk indicators (KRIs) that must be used by senior management to evaluate the effectiveness of an information security management system (ISMS).

32. C. A scripted process used to emulate user behavior

Explanation: Testing applications commonly involves the need to emulate usual user behaviors.

33. B. By testing restoration procedures

Explanation: Unless the ability to restore from backups successfully is tested routinely, no other activities around data retention have value.

34. A. It is performed to ensure that some systems will run at the alternative site.

Explanation: In a parallel test, some systems are run at the alternative site, and results are compared with how processing takes place at the prime site. This is to ensure the systems work at the alternate site and productivity is not affected.

35. D. Cell phone

Explanation: During a possible network intrusion, the best form of communication is out-of-band communications; it includes cell phones, telephones, and pagers.

36. B. Tripwire is a file integrity monitoring tool.

Explanation: Tripwire is one of the most well-known tools available for detecting unauthorized alterations to OS system files and software.

37. D. Root kit

Explanation: Root kits are software-based items that prevent users from seeing all items or directories on a computer.

38. A. Who, what, where, when, and how

Explanation: The following five items are required for proper chain of custody: who discovered it; what the evidence is; where it is being stored and where it was found; when it was discovered, seized, or analyzed; and how it has been collected, stored, or transported.

39. C. Computer crime

Explanation: Computer crime can be broadly defined as any criminal offense or activity that involves computers.

40. C. Digital watermarks

Explanation: The commercial application of steganography lies mainly in the use of digital watermarks.

41. A. It is illegal.

Explanation: Entrapment is considered illegal and unethical because it may encourage someone to commit a crime that was not intended.

42. B. It is legal.

Explanation: Enticement is measured legal because it may lure somebody into leaving some type of evidence after he or she has committed a crime.

43. B. Due care

Explanation: Due care is considered a reasonable person or corporation would practice under a given set of circumstances.

44. D. Physical surveillance

Explanation: Physical surveillance can be hidden cameras, closed-circuit TVs, security cameras, hardware key loggers, or security guards.

45. C. Direct evidence

Explanation: Direct evidence is provided by an oral or written statement; the witness provides this information using an eyewitness account.

46. B. To demonstrate evidence was properly controlled and handled

Explanation: For evidence to be admissible in court, it needs to be shown that it was properly controlled and handled.

47. B Fishing

Explanation: The correct term for social engineering conducted over digital communications means is phishing, not fishing.

48. D. User records auditing

Explanation: A records audit can verify that users have acknowledged acceptance of the policy.

49. C. Null hypothesis test

Explanation: The null hypothesis test is not used in disaster recovery and business continuity plan.

50. D. Major credit-card companies

Explanation: The major credit-card companies, such as MasterCard, Visa, and American Express, are responsible for Payment Card Industry Data Security Standard (PCI-DSS) standards.

Chapter 7

1. C. Both A and B

Explanation: Digital investigation are also called digital forensics, deals with collecting, preserving, and producing the evidence that pertains to computer crimes.

2. B. Detection

Explanation: Reporting must begin immediately upon detection of malicious activity.

3. A. Stakeholders

Explanation: Non-technical stakeholders including business and mission owners must be notified immediately of any serious incident and kept up to date as the incident handling process progresses.

4. D. Documentation

Explanation: The documentation process started when the report received.

5. B. EnCase forensic

Explanation: EnCase Forensic can be used to collect Digital Forensic Data

6. D. Regulatory

Explanation: A regulatory investigation is conducted by a regulating body, such as the Securities and Exchange Commission (SEC) or Financial Industry Regulatory Authority (FINRA), against an organization suspected of a violation.

7. A. NIDS

Explanation: Network-based intrusion detection (NIDS) consists of a separate device attached to a LAN that listens to all network traffic by using various methods to detect anomalous activity.

8. B. SIEM

Explanation: Correlation of security-related data is the primary utility provided by the SIEM.

9. C. Asset inventory

Explanation: Asset inventory helps organizations to protect physical assets from theft, maintain software licensing compliance, and account for the inventory.

10. C. It must be reliable

Explanation: For evidence to be admissible, it must be relevant, complete, sufficient, and reliable to the case.

11. C. A user should need to know to access specific resources, and least privilege should be implemented to ensure only accesses the resources need to know.

Explanation: There is a distinctive difference between the two; the need to know focuses on permissions and the ability to access information, whereas the least privilege focuses on privileges.

12. B. Preventing fraud

Explanation: Job rotation and separation of duties policies help prevent fraud.

13. C. IDS

Explanation: Intrusion Detection Systems (IDSs) provide only passive responses, such as notifying administrators of a suspected attack.

14. B. Software licensing

Explanation: One important term when dealing with operational security is keeping track of software licensing.

15. C. 7

Explanation: (ISC)² has prescribed seven phases in the incident management process: detect, respond, mitigate, report, recover, remediate, and learn.

16. B. Sandboxing

Explanation: Sandboxing is a technique where application developers may test the code in a virtualized environment that is isolated from production systems.

17. A. Resilience

Explanation: Resilience is the ability to recover quickly. With site resilience, if Site 1 goes down, Site 2 quickly and seamlessly comes operational.

18. C. Deploy all patches

Explanation: Only required patches should be deployed to an organization will not deploy all patches.

19. B. Vulnerability scanner

Explanation: Vulnerability scanners are used to check systems for known issues and are part of an overall vulnerability management program.

20. D. Simulation

Explanation: A simulation is a simulated disaster in which teams must go through their documented recovery plans. Simulations are very helpful to validate the detailed recovery plans, and the teams gain experience by performing recovery operations.

21. B. RAID 0

Explanation: RAID 0 provides only striping and is simply used for performance. It offers no additional data redundancy or resiliency.

22. A. Recovery Time Objective (RPO) and Work Recovery Time (WRT)

Explanation: The Recovery Time Objective (RTO) and Work Recovery Time (WRT) are used to calculate the Maximum Tolerable Downtime. RTO + WRT = MTD.

23. A. Business Continuity Plan (BCP)

Explanation: Business Continuity Planning develops a long-term plan to ensure the continuity of business operations.

24. D. Recovery Point Objective (RPO)

Explanation: The Recovery Point Objective (RPO) is the moment in time in which data must be recovered and made available to users to resume business operations.

25. C. The Mean Time to Repair (MTTR)

Explanation: The Mean Time to Repair (MTTR) describes how long it will take to recover a failed system.

26. C. RAID

Explanation: Redundant Array of Inexpensive Disks (RAID) provides fault tolerance for hard drives and can improve system performance.

27. B. Clustering

Explanation: Clustering provides for availability and scalability. It groups physically dissimilar systems and combines them logically, which helps to provide immunity to faults and improves performance.

28. C. Partial backup

Explanation: A backup can be a partial backup; it does not essentially mean that it backs up all the files that have been modified since the last time a backup process was run.

29. D. Differential process

Explanation: A differential process backs up the files that have been modified since the last full backup.

30. A. Determine the cause of the disaster.

Explanation: Determining the cause of the disaster is the first step of the damage assessment.

31. C. Declare a disaster.

Explanation: The final step in a damage assessment is to declare a disaster. After information from the damage assessment is gathered and assessed.

32. A. Damage assessment team

Explanation: Damage assessment team is responsible for determining the scope and severity of the damage caused.

33. C. Salvage team

Explanation: The salvage team is responsible for starting the recovery of the original site.

34. B 28 hours

Explanation: In this scenario, 28 hours is the RTO value.

35. C. Maximum tolerable downtime

Explanation: The Recovery Point Objective (RPO) is the acceptable amount of data loss measured in time.

36. A. Complete

Explanation: Evidence that is complete presents the whole truth.

37. B. Reliable

Explanation: Evidence that is reliable must be consistent with the facts.

38. C Recovery point objective

Explanation: The recovery point objective (RPO) is the acceptable amount of data loss measured in time.

39. C. Investigation

Explanation: Investigation involves the proper collection of relevant data during the incident response process and includes analysis, interpretation, reaction, and recovery.

40. D. RAID level 10

Explanation: RAID level 10 is associated with striping and mirroring.

41. C. RAID level 5

Explanation: RAID level 5 is the most commonly used mode and employs block-level striping and interleaving parity across all disks.

42. B. Software licensing

Explanation: Licensing is dealing with software.

43. B. Response

Explanation: Response is not the type of protection control.

44. C. Deterrent

Explanation: Deterrent controls are used to discourage security violations.

45. D. Interleave parity

Explanation: RAID level 5 indicates interleave parity.

46. A. Negligence

Explanation: Negligence is the number-one cause of intellectual property loss.

47. B. Warning banner

Explanation: Warning banner is an example of a technical deterrent.

48. D IDS

Explanation: IDS is an example of a technical detective.

49. D. Confidential operations

Explanation: According to the TCSEC definitions, Confidential operations is not a valid level.

50. A. Data remanence

Explanation: Data remanence is information that may remain on computer media after it has been deleted.

Chapter 8

1. C. V-shaped

Explanation: the V-shaped model is based on the waterfall model.

2. B. The spiral model

Explanation: The spiral model is the only valid software development methodology listed.

3. C. Capability Maturity Model

Explanation: The goal of the Software Capability Maturity Model(CMM) is to develop a methodical framework for creating quality software that lets measurable and repeatable results.

4. D. Defined

Explanation: Level 3: Defined Processes and procedures are designed and followed during the project.

5. B. Level 5: Optimizing

Explanation: Level 5: Optimizing is a model of continuous improvement for the development cycle.

6. A. Information security

Explanation: The three elements of the DevOps model are software development, quality assurance, and IT operations.

7. C. Request control

Explanation: The request control offers an organized framework in which users can request modifications, managers can conduct cost/benefit analysis, and developers can prioritize activities.

8. B. Code repositories

Explanation: Code repositories such as GitHub, Bitbucket, and SourceForge also provide version control, bug tracking, web hosting, release management, and communications functions that support software development.

9. C. Configuration audit

Explanation: Configuration audit is a portion of the configuration management process rather than the change control process.

10. A. The practice of incorporating development, IT, and quality assurance (QA) staff into software development projects.

Explanation: DevOps is a type of integrated product team (IPT) that focuses on three technologies: software development, IT operations, and quality assurance.

11. D. Both B and C

Explanation: After the development, testing and releasing of product, the next step of the process is to provide operational support and maintenance of the released product.

12. A. During requirements development

Explanation: The security should be implemented at the first conceivable phase of a project. Requirements are gathered and developed at the beginning of a project, which is project initiation. The other answers are steps that follow this phase, and security should be integrated right from the beginning instead of in the middle or at the end.

13. B. Mitigation

Explanation: When risk has been identified, a mitigation strategy should be created to avoid that risk.

14. D. All of the above

Explanation: Security controls must be considered at all points of the SDLC process.

15. A. Capability Maturity Model Integration

Explanation: The Software Capability Maturity Model (CMM) is a maturity framework for evaluating and improving the software development process.

16. D. Configuration Management

Explanation: Configuration Management is the process used to record all configuration changes to hardware and software.

17. C. MITRE

Explanation: The MITRE organization publishes a list of the Top 25 Most Dangerous Software Errors that can cause weaknesses and vulnerabilities in an application.

18. B. Agile

Explanation: Agile development emphasizes efficiency and iterations during the development process. Agile focuses on user stories to work through the development process.

19. D. Disposal phase

Explanation: Disposal phase is not listed in system security life cycle.

20. A. OWASP

Explanation: The Open Web Application Security Project (OWASP) has published a short list of security standards that organizations have adopted, most notably the Payment Card Industry Data Security Standard (PCI DSS).

21. D. Cross-site scripting (XSS)

Explanation: XSS is a third-party execution of web scripting languages, such as JavaScript, within the security context of a trusted site.

22. B. Entity integrity

Explanation: Entity integrity means each tuple has a unique primary key that is not empty.

23. C. Referential integrity

Explanation: Referential integrity means that every foreign key in a secondary table matches a primary key in the parent table.

24. C. DevOps

Explanation: DevOps is a more agile development and support model, where developers directly support operations.

25. C. Capability Maturity Model Integration

Explanation: Capability Maturity Model Integration (CMMI) for development is a comprehensive, integrated set of guidelines for developing products and software.

26. B. System development life cycle

Explanation: System development life cycle (SDLC) addresses how a system should be developed and maintained throughout its life cycle and does not violate process improvement.

27. A. ISO/IEC 27002

Explanation: ISO/IEC 27002 is an international standard created by the International Organization for Standardization (ISO) and the International Electrotechnical Commission (IEC) that outlines how to create and maintain an organizational Information Security Management System (ISMS).

28. B. Signature-based detection

Explanation: Signature-based detection uses signatures to identify malicious software or activity patterns before they are executed in the operating system.

29. D. Heuristic detection

Explanation: Heuristic detection analyzes the overall structure of the executable code, evaluates the coded instructions and logic functions.

30. B. Developing and testing software best suitable to the deployment environment

Explanation: Integrated Product Team (IPT) for software development is designed for developing and testing software that best suited to the deployment environment.

31. C. Controller server instructs infected systems to send spam to mail servers.

Explanation: The last step in the use of a botnet to send spam is the controller server instructing the infected systems to send out spam messages to mail servers.

32. B. DOM-based

Explanation: DOM is the standard structure layout to represent HTML and XML documents in the browser.

33. A. The structured database management system

Explanation: The structured database management system model is the invalid type.

34. D. Constructive

Explanation: The three valid types of application controls are preventive, corrective, and detective.

35. B. Object-oriented interfaces

Explanation: Object-oriented interfaces are part of object-oriented database management systems.

36. A. Initiating, repeatable, defined, managed, optimizing

Explanation: The software Capability Maturity Model (CMM) has the following order of maturity levels: 1. Initial, 2. Repeatable, 3. Defined 4. Managed 5. Optimizing

37. A. Audit logs are collected but not analyzed.

Explanation: The most common problems with audit logs is that they are collected but not analyzed.

38. C. Hierarchical

Explanation: A hierarchical database integrates related records and fields into a logical tree structure.

39. D. Data warehousing

Explanation: A data warehouse is used for data storage and can combine data from multiple sources.

40. A. A form of insurance

Explanation: Software escrow is a form of insurance.

41. D. The NIST's National Software Reference Library

Explanation: The NIST's National Software Reference Library was the only term that is not assessing the acquired software.

42. A. Fuzz testing

Explanation: Fuzz testing is a software testing technique that provides invalid, unexpected, or random data to the input interfaces of a program.

43. C. Tuples and attributes

Explanation: In a relational database, a row represents a tuple whereas a column represents an attribute.

44. A. Entity integrity

Explanation: Entity integrity guarantees that primary key values uniquely identify the tuples.

45. A. Behavior blocking

Explanation: Behavior blocking allows suspicious code to execute within the operating system and watches its interactions looking for suspicious activities.

46. A. Second-order vulnerability

Explanation: Second-order vulnerability is another name for a persistent XSS vulnerability which targets websites that allow users to input data that is stored in a database.

47. D. Unit testing

Explanation: Unit testing involves testing an individual component in a controlled environment to validate data structure, logic, and boundary conditions.

48. A. Acceptance testing

Explanation: Acceptance testing is carried out to ensure that the code meets customer requirements.

49. A. Level 1

Explanation: At level 1 of the CMM, processes likely to be variable and depend heavily on institutional knowledge.

50. B. CORBA

Explanation: Common Object Request Broker Architecture (CORBA) is vendor-independent middleware technology.

About Our Products

Other Network & Security related products from IPSpecialist LTD are:

- CCNA Routing & Switching Technology Workbook
- CCNA Security Technology Workbook
- CCNA Service Provider Technology Workbook
- CCDA Technology Workbook
- CCDP Technology Workbook
- CCNP Route Technology Workbook
- CCNP Switch Technology Workbook
- CCNP Troubleshoot Technology Workbook
- CCNP Security SENSS Technology Workbook
- CCNP Security SIMOS Technology Workbook
- CCNP Security SITCS Technology Workbook
- CCNP Security SISAS Technology Workbook
- CompTIA Network+ Technology Workbook
- CompTIA Security+ Technology Workbook
- EC-Council CEH v10 Technology Workbook

Upcoming products are:

- CCNA CyberOps SECFND Technology Workbook
- CCNA CyberOps SECOPS Technology Workbook
- Certified Block Chain Expert Technology Workbook
- Certified Cloud Security Professional (CCSP) Technology Workbook
- Certified Application Security Engineer (Java) Technology Workbook
- Certified Application Security Engineer (.Net) Technology Workbook
- Certified Information Security Manager Technology Workbook
- Certified Information Systems Auditor Technology Workbook

Note from the Author:

Reviews are gold to authors! If you have enjoyed this book and helped you along certification, would you consider rating it and reviewing it?

Link to Product Page:

www.ingramcontent.com/pod-product-compliance
Lightning Source LLC
Chambersburg PA
CBHW060150060326
40690CB00018B/4058